The Plutarch Project

Volume Five (Revised)

Alexander and Timoleon

by

Anne E. White

ISBN 978-1-990258-18-3

CONTENTS

Introduction

These notes, and the accompanying text, are prepared for the use of individual students and small groups following a twelve-week term.

The text is a free mixture of Thomas North's 1579 translation of Plutarch's *Lives of the Noble Greeks and Romans* and John Dryden's 1683 translation. (Dryden for clarity, North for character.) Omissions have been made for length and suitability, for the intended age group. Those using audio versions or other translations will want to preview those editions for "necessary omissions."

Some lessons are divided into two or three sections. These can be read all at once or used throughout the week.

Using the Lesson Material

Each study contains explanatory material before the first lesson. A little at the beginning may be useful to stir interest in the study, but it is not meant to be given all in one dose! The information may help as you introduce later lessons, or it may be used to answer students' questions.

I encourage you to make the lessons your own. Use the questions that are the most meaningful to you. Remember that Charlotte Mason was satisfied with "Proper names are written on the blackboard, and then the children narrate what they have listened to."

She also emphasized the importance of recapitulation, which can have two meanings: beginning each lesson by remembering what has gone before; or recalling something already known, and emphasizing particular points at the end of a lesson, which (again) should help with the next one.

Examination Questions

The two studies in this volume include suggestions for end-of-term examinations, with separate questions for each term of the *Life of Alexander*. The questions were drawn from original P.N.E.U. programmes.

Alexander III of Macedon

(356-323 B.C.)

> Another time also when he was in Spain, reading the
> history of Alexander's acts, when he had read it, he
> was sorrowful a good while after, and then burst out
> in weeping. His friends, seeing that, marvelled what
> should be the cause of his sorrow. "Do ye not think,"
> said he, "that I have good cause to be heavy, when
> King Alexander being no older than myself is now,
> had in old time won so many nations and countries:
> and that I hitherunto have done nothing worthy of
> myself?"(Plutarch's *Life of Julius Caesar*)

Alexander the Great may be the best known, and the most
romanticized, of Plutarch's biographical subjects. His story has been
examined and debated for over two thousand years, by everyone from
Oxford scholars to schoolchildren making stop-motion videos.
Although Alexander lived only a few hundred years before this account
was written, and historians had already described his life in detail,
Plutarch still had to deal with unconfirmed stories and questionable
"facts," from the legends around Alexander's birth to his mysterious
death. However, Plutarch's aims were slightly different: he was

concerned with character, moral choices, and problems of leadership and government. Does power always corrupt? Should kings live in safety and luxury, or should they fight on the front lines? What motivates greatness? (What *is* greatness?)

Who was Alexander?

Alexander was born into the Macedonian royal family in 356 B.C. For many years, the dominant political power in Europe and the Middle East had been the Persian empire; but Persia's strength had weakened, and its subjects were now becoming rebellious. Alexander's father, Philip II of Macedon, became king soon after his son was born, and he was credited with reforming and strengthening the army (using the famous phalanx formation). He planned to combine Macedon's military power with that of the Greek city-states, and to attack Persia (**Lesson Two**).

Philip's assassination in 336 left that ambition unfulfilled. However, his son Alexander spent the next thirteen years conquering a previously undreamed-of share of the world.

Is it Macedon or Macedonia? Were the Macedonians Greeks?

The names are used interchangeably. Macedonia, or Macedon, was a kingdom in the northeastern part of mainland Greece. The Macedonians were Greek in many respects, such as religious beliefs; but they valued their distinct heritage and identity.

What is meant by "barbarous?"

The word "barbarous" meant "foreign" or "not Greek." It carried overtones of "strange," but it did not imply "savage or cruel."

People in this Story

Alexander's Teachers

Aristotle: "The Father of Western Philosophy" was hired by King Philip to teach Alexander (and other young men) subjects such as natural philosophy (science) and rhetoric.

Leonidas of Epirus: Alexander's schoolmaster and a relative of his mother Olympias.

Lysimachus of Acarnania: Alexander's second-place tutor, who suggested the nicknames "Phoenix" for himself, "Achilles" for Alexander, and "Peleus" for Philip.

Anaxarchus: one of the philosophers called to counsel Alexander during his grief after killing Cleitus (**Lesson Seventeen**).

Alexander's Military Colleagues

Nearchus/Nearchos: Alexander's admiral and official explorer.

Parmenion/Parmenio: Philip's chief lieutenant, and later a general to Alexander. His eldest son was **Philotas**, a cavalry commander.

Perdiccas: one of Alexander's generals, later the head of the Imperial Army, and regent during the reign of Alexander's half-brother **Arrhidaeus** (see note below).

Antipater was born in 397 B.C. He appears in **Lesson Three** as "one of Alexander's chiefest servants." Antipater was an advisor and friend to Alexander, and to Alexander's mother **Olympias**, during the early years of his reign, and he acted as regent (substitute ruler) when Alexander was in Persia and India. His friendship with Alexander gradually deteriorated, due to mistrust and jealousy.

Antipater's son **Cassander** is not mentioned until **Lesson Twenty-Three**. He lived from about 350-297 B.C., and later became king of Macedon. As a boy, he had been a student of Aristotle along with Alexander.

Plutarch also mentions another of Antipater's sons, **Iolaus**, who was suspected of poisoning Alexander.

Antigonus Monopthalmus (or "Antigonus with One Eye"):
Those who have read the *Life of Demetrius* will remember Antigonus, the father of Demetrius and one of Alexander's generals.

Seleucus I Nicator was a general in Alexander's army who eventually ruled much of the Middle East. He is, however, barely mentioned in this story. **Ptolemy I Soter**, another general, became ruler of Egypt after Alexander's death. He is also not mentioned much here.

The Wives and Children of Alexander

Alexander had a complicated list of marriages and other relationships. The most important to know are his wives **Statira** (also spelled **Stateira**) and **Roxane** (also **Roxana** or **Rhoxane**). A third wife was named **Parysatis**. Alexander is believed to have been the father of at least two sons, including **Alexander IV** who was born to **Roxane** after his death.

Other People

Cleopatra Eurydice was a stepmother to Alexander.

Arrhidaeus: Alexander's half-brother became King Philip Arrhidaeus III of Macedon in 323 B.C. According to historians, he was not considered fully capable of ruling, possibly due to a childhood injury. He was put to death by Alexander's mother **Olympias**.

Hephaestion: one of Alexander's closest friends. Some thought that Alexander's grief over Hephaestion's death hastened his own end.

Craterus: another of Alexander's generals

Darius III: king of Persia at the time

Harpalus: Those who have read the *Life of Demosthenes* will remember Alexander's friend Harpalus, whose visit to Athens (while escaping Alexander's anger) caused trouble for Demosthenes. (Those events are mentioned briefly here in **Lesson Fifteen**.)

How P.N.E.U. teachers taught *Alexander*

There are a few mentions of the *Life of Alexander* in Charlotte Mason's writings and in early *Parents' Review* articles. Interestingly, it appears under the subjects of both Narration/Language and History, but not Citizenship (its place in later P.N.E.U. programmes).

Two lesson plans for passages in *Alexander* appear in Appendix V of *School Education*, "How Oral Lessons are Used." The first lesson is designed to take twenty minutes, and the second, thirty; the first says that it is intended for students with an average age of ten, and the other is for students aged eight or nine (below the usual age for Plutarch in the later programmes).

The first lesson plan (included below) is the simplest. Note **Step 2**, which sounds like Charlotte Mason's Bible lessons as described in *Home Education*, giving students an overview of the story before reading the whole thing. Elsewhere, we are directed to read a passage without much preamble and let the students take from it what they can, rather than kill the story with too much talk. However, telling the story-before-the-story is a way to unlock difficult passages, or those that include significant events such as famous battles.

> **Step 1.** Connect with the last lesson by questioning the children. They read last time stories illustrating Alexander's graciousness and tact.
>
> **Step 2.** Tell the children shortly the substance of what I am going to read to them, letting them find any places mentioned, in their maps.
>
> **Step 3.** Read to the children about three pages, dealing with the luxury of the Macedonians, Alexander's march to Bactria, and the death of Darius. Read this slowly and distinctly, and "into" the children as much as possible.
>
> **Step 4.** Ask the children in turn to narrate, each narrating a part of what was read.

The second lesson is longer, but as it is also included in *School Education*, I will not repeat it here. This was intended as a first lesson on Alexander, "a fresh hero." After discussing a few details about place and time, the class read and narrated the story of Alexander's taming of Bucephalus. They were asked to list "the qualities which go to make a hero," and looked for examples of those qualities in the story. The teacher pointed out that Alexander himself admired heroic qualities (seen in his admiration for *The Iliad*), and she stressed the impact of Alexander's life on the world.

Charlotte Mason notes, "These [oral] lessons are always expansions or illustrations or summaries of some part of the scholars' current book-work." In other words, they were not written to show how every lesson should be studied, including Plutarch; but as reminders that we teach with "things and ideas," and as suggestions of ways that books written for adults may be used with young students, without either patronizing them or confusing them with irrelevancies.

Maps and Alexander's World

Because Alexander's story covers such a broad range of places, it is helpful to refer to maps in a historical atlas or the online equivalent. This study contains notes under the heading "On the Map."

Top Vocabulary Terms in *Alexander*

If you recognize these words, you are well on your way to mastering the vocabulary of this story. (They will not be noted in the lessons.)

1. **acquaint:** This can mean either "to become used to, familiar with" or "to share information."

2. **buckler:** shield, in Dryden's translation. North prefers **target**.

3. **choler:** anger, temper

4. **divers:** several, various

5. **familiars:** close friends

6. **footmen:** foot soldiers, infantry, sometimes called "foot." **Horsemen** are the cavalry, or simply "horse."

7. **lance, javelin, dart:** a long pointed weapon; spear

8. **meet:** proper, just. When Philip said his son should have a kingdom that was "meet" for him, he meant "large enough, sufficient."

9. **physic:** medicine, both the science and the potion. An expert in medicine is a **physician**.

10. **soothsayer:** someone who can predict the future. Soothsayers often specialized in the interpretation of **omens**, such as an owl landing on one's roof.

11. **spoil** or **spoils:** loot, treasure, plunder; especially from a defeated enemy. Most of these words can be used either as nouns ("they took the loot") or verbs ("they spoiled the camp").

12. **stay:** Often used to mean delay, detain, stop. It can also be used in the more familiar sense of "remain" (stay here).

13. **strange:** usually means "foreign," but sometimes it just means "strange." Soldiers that are **strangers** are often foreign **mercenaries** (soldiers employed by any army that will pay them).

Lesson One

Introduction

What do your students know about Alexander the Great? Do they have any ideas about how he earned that title?

In two sample lessons included in Charlotte Mason's book *School Education* (see the introductory notes for this study), an unnamed teacher describes Alexander's "wisdom, valour, and self-reliance," and his "love of simplicity, generosity, and kindness to his men." She suggests that Alexander had a gift of prudence, and that he knew how to put important things first. As you read this *Life*, you may agree that those traits accurately describe Alexander; or you may argue that his values changed during his lifetime. (Did Alexander retain his love of simplicity, or was it destroyed when he began to dress like a Persian?) Or you may disagree with them completely. (Was Alexander truly wise and great, or not?)

Vocabulary

Olympic games: a festival held every fourth year, including sports competitions, music, and religious rituals

had brought him a son: had given birth to a son

invincible: unconquerable

stature and personage: personal appearance

for that he would be drawn…: Alexander would allow no other artist to draw him

counterfeit: copy

hasty: hot-tempered

chaste: moderate in behaviour (such as not overeating)

essay: attempt

playing at the staff: fighting with staffs or sticks (like Robin Hood)

ought worth: worth anything

churlish: mean-spirited, rude

yerk: jerk, kick

what wilt thou forfeit for thy folly: What are you willing to bet?

jeopardize: bet, wager

voice a-good: Dryden, "in a commanding voice"

was lighted from: alighted from, got down from

People

Parmenion, Queen Olympias: see introductory notes

Lysippus (Lysippos), Apelles: artists who sculpted and painted Alexander

Leonidas, Lysimachus: Alexander's tutors (see introductory notes)

Historic Occasions

357 B.C.: Marriage of Olympias and Philip (Alexander's parents)

356 B.C.: Birth of Alexander

346 B.C.: Alexander tamed Bucephalus

On the Map

On a map of Europe and Asia, preferably one representing the fourth century B.C., locate Macedon, Greece, and the Persian Empire.

Potidaea: a city in northern **Greece**

Illyria (Illyrians): a region of the **Balkan Peninsula**

Asia (or Asia Minor): the region of the **Anatolian Peninsula** (part of modern-day Turkey)

Acarnania: a region of west-central Greece

Reading

Part One

[omission: omens pertaining to Alexander's birth]

Shortly after King Philip had won the city of **Potidaea**, three messengers came to him the same day that brought him great news. The first was that **Parmenion** had won a notable battle of the **Illyrians**: the second, that his horse had won the course at the **Olympic games**: and the third, that his wife **had brought him a son** called Alexander. Philip being marvellous glad to hear these news, the **soothsayers** did make his joy yet greater: assuring him that his son which was born with three victories all together should be **invincible**.

Now for his **stature and personage**, the statues and images made of him by **Lysippus** do best declare it, **for that he would be drawn**

of no man but him only. Divers of his successors and friends did afterwards **counterfeit** his image, but that excellent workman Lysippus only, of all other the chiefest, hath perfectly drawn and resembled Alexander's manner of holding his neck, somewhat hanging down towards the left side, and also the sweet look and cast of his eyes. But when **Apelles** painted Alexander, holding lightning in his hand, he did not show his fresh colour, but made him somewhat [darker] than his face indeed was: for naturally he had a very fair white colour mingled also with red, which chiefly appeared in his face and in his breast.

[omission]

This natural heat that Alexander had, made him (as it appeareth) to be given to drink, and to be **hasty**. Even from his childhood they saw that he was given to be **chaste** *[omission]*. But on the other side, the ambition and desire he had of honour, showed a certain greatness of mind and noble courage, passing his years. For he was not (as his father Philip) desirous of all kind of glory: who took care to have the victories of his racing chariots at the Olympic games engraved on his coin. For when he [Alexander] was asked one day (because he was swift of foot) whether he would **essay** to run for victory at the Olympic games: "I could be content," said he, "if I might run with kings." And yet to speak generally, he misliked all such contention for games. For it seemeth that he utterly misliked all wrestling and other exercise for prize, where men did use all their strength: but otherwise he himself made certain festival days and games of prize, for common stage-players, musicians, and singers, and for the very poets also. He delighted also in hunting of divers kinds of beasts, and **playing at the staff**.

Part Two

Ambassadors being sent on a time from the king of Persia, whilst his father was in some journey out of his realm: Alexander, familiarly entertaining of them, so won them with his courteous entertainment (for he used no childish questions unto them, nor asked them trifling matters, but what distance it was from one place to another, and which way they went into the high countries of **Asia**, and of the king of Persia himself, how he was towards his enemies, and what power he had), that they were struck with admiration of him, and looked upon the ability so much famed of Philip to be nothing in comparison with the forwardness and high purpose that appeared thus early in his son.

For when they brought him news that his father had taken some famous city, or had won some great battle, he was nothing glad to hear it, but would say to his playfellows: "Sirs, my father will have all, I shall have nothing left me to conquer with you, that shall be **ought worth**." For being more bent upon action and glory than either upon pleasure or riches, he esteemed all that he should receive from his father as a diminution and prevention of his own future achievements; and would have chosen rather to succeed to a kingdom involved in troubles and wars, which would have afforded him frequent exercise of his courage, and a large field of honour, than to one already flourishing and settled, where his inheritance would be an inactive life, and the mere enjoyment of wealth and luxury.

He had divers men appointed him (as it is to be supposed) to bring him up: as schoolmasters, governors, and grooms of his chamber to attend upon him: and among those, **Leonidas** was the chiefest man that had the government and charge of him, a man of a severe disposition, and a kinsman also unto **Queen Olympias**. He misliked to be called a master or tutor, though it be an office of good charge; whereupon the others called him Alexander's governor, because he was a noble man, and allied to the prince. But he that bore the name of his schoolmaster was **Lysimachus**, an **Acarnanian** born, who had no other manner of civility in him saving that he called himself "Phoenix," Alexander "Achilles," and Philip "Peleus"; and, therefore, he was well thought of, and was the second person next unto Leonidas.

Part Three

At what time Philonicus the Thessalian had brought Bucephalus the horse to sell unto King Philip, asking thirteen talents, they went into the field to ride him. The horse was found so rough and **churlish** that the riders said he would never do service, for he would let no man get up on his back, nor abide any of the gentlemen's voices about King Philip; but would **yerk** out at them. Thereupon, Philip being afraid, commanded them to carry him away as a wild beast, and altogether unprofitable: the which they would have done, had not Alexander that stood by said, "Gods, what a horse do they turn away, for lack of skill and heart to handle him." Philip heard what he said but held his peace. Alexander, oft repeating his words, seemed to be sorry that they should send back the horse again. "Why," said Philip, "dost thou control them that have more experience than thou, and that know better than thou how to handle a horse?" Alexander answered, "And yet methinks I should handle him better than all they have done." "But if thou canst not, no more than they," replied Philip: "**what wilt thou forfeit for thy folly?**" "I am content," (quoth Alexander) "to **jeopardize** the price of the horse." Every man laughed to hear his answer, and the wager was laid between them. Then ran Alexander to the horse and took him by the bridle and turned him towards the sun. It seemed that he had marked (as I suppose) how mad the horse was to see his own shadow, which was ever before him in his eye, as he stirred to and fro. Then Alexander speaking gently to the horse, and clapping him on the back with his hand, till he had left his fury and snorting: softly let fall his cloak from him, and lightly leaping on his back, got up without any danger, and holding the reins of the bridle hard, without striking or stirring the horse, made him to be gentle enough. Then when he saw that the fury of the horse was past, and that he began to gallop, he put him to his full career, and laid on spurs and **voice a-good**. Philip at the first with fear beholding his son's agility, lest he should take some hurt, said never a word: but when he saw him readily turn the horse at the end of his career, in a bravery for that he had done, all the lookers on gave a shout for joy. The father, on the other side (as they say), fell a-weeping for joy. And when Alexander **was lighted from** the horse, he said unto him, kissing his head: "O son, thou must needs have a realm that is meet for thee, for Macedon will not hold thee."

After this, considering Alexander to be of a temper easy to be led to his duty by reason, but by no means to be compelled, Philip always endeavoured to persuade rather than to command or to force him to anything.

Narration and Discussion

Retell the story of Alexander and Bucephalus. Why do you think this story has been told so often? What does it say about Alexander's character, even as a boy?

"He desired no riches nor pleasure, but wars and battles." Should we admire Alexander's determination to make his country great?

For older students and further thought: How does the last sentence compare Philip's education of Alexander to Alexander's handling of the horse? Is this a useful philosophy for those who lead or train others?

Creative narration #1: Have a reporter interview young Alexander (or some of the people around him). What is he most proud of? What are his goals?

Creative narration #2: Students interested in art may want to discuss the problems of portraiture. How do you know when someone has been captured "accurately" with paints, or with a camera? (Older students who have read *Daughter of Time* by Josephine Tey might consider the copies of famous portraits that the main character examines, and the conclusions he comes to.)

> He pushed the portrait at her.
>
> What did she think of it? If that man were her patient what would be her verdict?
>
> 'Liver,' she said crisply, and bore away the tray in heel-tapping protest, all starch and blonde curls.
>
> (*Daughter of Time*)

Lesson Two

Introduction

As Alexander grew up, he received his schooling, put down a rebellion, and suddenly became king of Macedon. He seemed to have had the perfect education and training, but he was still very young. Was he prepared to handle this new role?

Vocabulary

affiance: trust

honourable stipend: generous pay

professed to reserve for oral communication to the initiated: taught only to advanced students

ambitious humour: desire to be greater than all others

published and not published: Aristotle explained that yes, he had published the metaphysical teaching which had been only for the privileged; but there was no danger in making that knowledge public, because most people wouldn't understand it anyway.

memoranda: reminders; something to refresh one's knowledge

corrected: edited

casket copy: see **Lesson Nine** for an explanation of the "casket"

allured: tempted, persuaded

People

Aristotle, Harpalus, etc.: see introductory notes

Pausanius of Orestis: one of Philip's bodyguards. The story of his personal grudge has been told by other historians, but it cannot be repeated here. Briefly, he blamed Philip for not avenging an insult that he had received. The mystery around the murder seems to be who it was that persuaded Pausanias to carry it out; even Alexander was not above suspicion.

Historic Occasions

343 B.C.: Aristotle became Alexander's teacher

339 B.C.: Philip besieged Byzantium

338 B.C.: Battle of Chaeronea

Summer, 336 B.C.: Darius III became king of Persia

October, 336 B.C.: Alexander became king of Macedon

On the Map

Stagira: a Greek city, known as the birthplace of Aristotle

Mieza: a village in Macedonia

Byzantium (Byzantines): the city (now in Turkey) that became Constantinople and later Istanbul

Medarians: a **Thracian** tribe

Chaeronea: a town in **Boeotia**, Greece

Thebes (Thebans): a city in Boeotia

Reading

Part One

Now Philip put no great **affiance** in the schoolmasters of music and humanity for the instruction and education of his son whom he had appointed to teach him; but he thought rather that he needed men of greater learning than their capacities would reach unto; and that as Sophocles sayeth,

> He needed many reins, and many bits at once. *[Dryden: "the bridle and the rudder too"]*

He sent for **Aristotle** (the greatest philosopher in his time, and best learned) to teach his son, unto whom he gave **honourable stipend**. For he repeopled his native city **Stagira**, which he had caused to be demolished a little before, and restored all the citizens, who were in exile or slavery, to their habitations.

As a place for the pursuit of their studies and exercise, he assigned the Temple of the Nymphs, near **Mieza**, where, to this very day, they show you Aristotle's stone seats, and the shady walks which he was wont to frequent.

It is thought that Alexander did not only learn of Aristotle moral philosophy and humanity, but also that he heard of him something of those more abstruse and profound theories which these philosophers, by the very names they gave them, **professed to reserve for oral communication to the initiated,** or else those which are kept from common knowledge: which sciences they did not commonly teach. For when Alexander was in Asia, hearing that Aristotle had put out certain books of that matter, he wrote to him, using very plain language to him in behalf of philosophy, the following letter:

> "Alexander unto Aristotle, greeting: Thou hast not
> done well to put forth your books of oral doctrine:
> for wherein shall we excel others, if those things
> which thou hast secretly taught us, be made
> common to all? I do wish thee to understand that I
> had rather excel others in excellency of knowledge,
> than in greatness of power. Farewell."

Whereunto Aristotle, to pacify this his **ambitious humour,** wrote unto him again that these books were both **published, and not published.** For to say truly, his books on metaphysics are written in a style which makes them useless for ordinary teaching, and instructive only in the way of **memoranda,** for those who have already been conversant in that sort of learning.

Doubtless also it was to Aristotle that he owed the inclination he had, not to the theory only, but likewise to the practice of the art of medicine. For when any of his friends were sick, he would often prescribe them their course of diet, and medicines proper to their disease, as we may find in his epistles. He was naturally a great lover of all kinds of learning and reading; and Onesicritus informs us that he constantly laid Homer's *Iliad,* according to the copy **corrected** by Aristotle, called the "**casket copy,**" with his dagger under his pillow, declaring that he esteemed it a perfect portable treasure of all military virtue and knowledge. And *[later in his life],* when he was in the high countries of Asia, where he could not readily come by other books, he wrote unto **Harpalus** to send them to him. (Harpalus sent him the histories of Philistus, with divers tragedies of Euripides, Sophocles, and Aeschylus, and certain hymns of Telestus and Philoxenus.)

Alexander did reverence Aristotle at the first, as his father, and so he termed him: because from his natural father he had life, but from him [Aristotle] the knowledge to live. But afterwards he suspected him somewhat, yet he did him no hurt, neither was he so friendly to him as he had been: whereby men perceived that he did not bear him the goodwill he was wont to do. This notwithstanding, he left not that zeal and desire he had to the study of philosophy, which he had learned from his youth, and still continued.

[short omission]

Part Two

When King Philip made war with the **Byzantines**, Alexander, being but sixteen years old, was left as his lieutenant in Macedon, with the custody and charge of his great seal. Not to sit idle, he subdued the **Medarians** which had rebelled against him; and having won their city by assault, he drove out the barbarous people, and made a colony of it of sundry nations, and called it Alexandropolis, to say, "the city of Alexander."

He was with his father at the Battle of **Chaeronea** against the Grecians, where it was reported that it was he that gave charge first of all upon the holy band of the **Thebans**. Furthermore, there was an old oak seen in my time, which the countrymen commonly call Alexander's Oak, because his tent or pavilion was fastened to it. And not far off are to be seen the graves of the Macedonians who fell in that battle.

For these causes, his father Philip loved him very dearly, and was glad to hear the Macedonians call Alexander king, and himself their captain *[Dryden: general]*. Howbeit the troubles that fell out in his court afterwards, by reason of Philip's new marriages and loves, bred great quarrel and strife amongst the women: for the mischief of dissension and jealousy of women doth separate the hearts of kings one from another. The chiefest cause was the sharpness of [Queen] Olympias, who, being a jealous woman, fretting, and of a revenging mind, did incense Alexander against his father.

[Omission: events and intrigue involving King Philip, his new second wife **Cleopatra***, his other son* **Arrhidaeus***, and a proposed royal wedding between Arrhidaeus and a Carian princess. When Alexander became involved in this*

tangle, Philip punished him by banishing several of his friends.]

Shortly after, **Pausanias**, [having a personal grudge against Philip], watched for his opportunity and murdered him. Of this murder, most men accused Olympias, who (as it is reported) **allured** this young man, having just cause of anger, to kill him. There was some sort of suspicion attached even to Alexander himself *[short omission]*. However, he took care to find out and punish the accomplices of the conspiracy severely; and [he] was very angry with Olympias for treating Cleopatra inhumanely in his absence.

Narration and Discussion

How did Philip recognize and encourage his son's special gifts?

How was Alexander able to accomplish so much before the age of twenty? (You may want to look up 1 Timothy 4:12.)

For older students: If you have read *The Iliad*, do you agree with Alexander's wholehearted admiration of that book? Do you have a book that has become your lifelong guide?

Lesson Three

Introduction

How should a young, ambitious king make the right impression on his country's friends and enemies? In Part One of this lesson, Alexander made a violent choice, but he wondered later if he had gone too far.

Part Two is a short and much lighter story which should provoke some discussion about material needs and desires.

Vocabulary

barbarous: see introductory notes

18

insolency: unfriendly attitude, rudeness

timorous: timid, cowardly

magnanimity: this usually means generosity of spirit; but here it means acting unwaveringly. Plutarch adds the phrase "to make them know he was a man."

truckle: bow down

Then did Alexander leave the Macedonians…: He allowed his soldiers to attack without restraint. [*Dryden: He presently applied himself to make them feel the last extremities of war.*]

made a sally: rushed out to attack

an attempt to gratify the hostility of his confederates: his excuse was that he needed to gain the confidence of the Phocians and Plataeans

those that had dissuaded…: those who had attempted to end the rebellion

mien and gait: manner and way of walking

celebration of the Mysteries: a time of religious observance

imputed: blamed

in his wine: when he was drunk

Bacchus: the Greek god of wine

People

Demosthenes: an orator in Athens who had spoken against Philip's aggression (see Plutarch's *Life of Demosthenes*)

Philotas and **Antipater:** see introductory notes

Pindar: a poet from Thebes

Diogenes of Sinope: a founder of Cynic philosophy (forerunner of Stoicism)

Historic Occasions

September, 335 B.C.: Fall of Thebes

On the Map

Alexander's army marched south to Thebes and Corinth.

> **Corinth:** the city-state located on the strip of land (**isthmus**) which
> divides Greece into its northern and southern parts

Reading

Part One

So he came to be king of Macedon at twenty years of age, and found
his realm greatly envied and hated of dangerous enemies, and every
way full of danger. For the **barbarous** nations that were near
neighbours unto Macedon were impatient of being governed by any
but their own native princes. Neither had Philip time enough to bridle
and pacify Greece, which he had conquered by force of arms: but
having a little altered the governments, he had through his **insolency**
left them all in great trouble and ready to rebel, for that they had not
long been acquainted to obey.

It seemed to the Macedonians a very critical time; and some would
have persuaded Alexander to give up all thought of retaining the
Grecians in subjection by force of arms, and rather to apply himself to
win back by gentle means the barbarous people that had rebelled
against him, and wisely to remedy these new stirs. But he rejected this
counsel as weak and **timorous**, and looked upon it to be more prudent
to secure himself by resolution and **magnanimity** than by seeming to
truckle to any, to encourage all to trample on him.

Thereupon, he straight quenched all the rebellion of the barbarous
people, invading them suddenly with his army, by the river Danube,
where in a great battle he overthrew Syrmus, king of the Triballians.
Furthermore, having intelligence that the **Thebans** had revolted, and
that the Athenians also were confederate with them: to make them
know that he was a man, he marched with his army through the pass

of Thermopylae, saying that to **Demosthenes**, who had called him "a child" while he was in Illyria and in the country of the Triballians, and "a youth" when he was in Thessaly, he would appear "a man" before the walls of Athens.

When he came with his army unto the gates of Thebes, he was willing to give those of the city occasion to repent themselves: and therefore demanded only Phoenix and Prothytes, authors of the rebellion. Furthermore, he proclaimed, by trumpet, pardon and safety unto all them that would yield unto him. The Thebans, on the other side, demanded of him **Philotas** and **Antipater,** two of his chiefest servants, and made the crier proclaim in the city that all such as would defend the liberty of Greece should join with them. **Then did Alexander leave the Macedonians at liberty to make war with all cruelty.**

The Thebans indeed defended themselves with a zeal and courage beyond their strength, being much outnumbered by their enemies. And on the other side also, when the garrison of the Macedonians, which were within the citadel, **made a sally** upon them and gave them charge in the rearward: then they, being environed of all sides, were slain in manner every one of them, their city taken, destroyed, and razed even to the hard ground. This he did, specially to make all the rest of the people of Greece afraid by example of this great calamity and misery of the Thebans, to the end that none of them should dare from thenceforth once to rise against him. He would cloak this cruelty of his under **an attempt to gratify the hostility of his confederates**. So that, except the priests, and some few who had heretofore been the friends and connections of the Macedonians, the family of the poet **Pindar**, and those who were known to have opposed the public vote for the war, all the rest, to the number of thirty thousand, were publicly sold for slaves; and it is computed that upwards of six thousand were put to the sword.

Part Two (optional)

Among the other calamities that befell the city, it happened that some **Thracian** soldiers, having broken into the house of a matron of high character and repute named Timoclea; their captain, after he had used violence with her *[omission]*, asked her if she knew of any money concealed; to which she readily answered she did, and bade him follow her into a garden, where she showed him a well into which, she told him, upon the taking of the city, she had thrown what she had of most value. The greedy Thracian presently stooping down to view the place where he thought the treasure lay, she came behind him and pushed him into the well, and then flung great stones in upon him, till she had killed him.

After which, when the solders led her away bound to Alexander, her very **mien and gait** showed her to be a woman of dignity, and of a mind no less elevated, not betraying the least sign of fear or astonishment. And when the king asked her who she was, "I am," said she, "the sister of Theagenes, who fought in the Battle of Chaeronea with your father Philip and fell there in command for the liberty of Greece." Alexander was so surprised, both at what she had done and what she said, that he could not choose but give her and her children their freedom to go whither they pleased.

Part Three

After this he received the Athenians into favour, although they had shown themselves so much concerned at the calamity of Thebes that out of sorrow they omitted the **celebration of the Mysteries**, and entertained those who escaped with all possible humanity. Whether it were, like the lion, that his passion was now satisfied, or that, after an example of extreme cruelty, he had a mind to appear merciful, it happened well for the Athenians; for he not only forgave them all past offences, but did also counsel them to look wisely to their doings, for their city one day should command all Greece, if he chanced to die.

Certain it is, too, that in aftertime he often repented of his severity to the Thebans, and his remorse had such influence on his temper as to make him ever after less rigorous to all others. He **imputed** also the murder of Cleitus, which he committed **in his wine** [**Lesson Seventeen**], and the unwillingness of the Macedonians to follow him against the Indians [**Lesson Twenty**], by which his enterprise and glory was left imperfect, to the wrath and vengeance of **Bacchus,** the protector of Thebes. And it was observed that whatsoever any Theban, who had the good fortune to survive this victory, asked of him, he was sure to grant without the least difficulty.

Part Four

Soon after, the Grecians, being assembled at the **Isthmus**, declared their resolution of joining with Alexander in the war against the Persians, and proclaimed him their general. While he stayed here, many public ministers and philosophers came from all parts to visit him and congratulated him on his election. He [expected] that **Diogenes of Sinope** (who dwelt at **Corinth**) would likewise come as the rest had done: but when he saw he made no reckoning of him, and that he kept still in the suburbs of Corinth, at a place called the Cranium, he went himself unto him, and found him laid all along in the sun.

When Diogenes saw so many coming towards him, he sat up a little, and looked full upon Alexander. Alexander courteously spoke unto him, and asked him if he lacked anything. "Yea," said he, "that I do: that thou stand out of my sun a little."

Alexander was so well pleased with this answer, and marvelled so much at the great boldness of this man, to see how small account he made of him: that when he went his way from him, Alexander's familiars laughing at Diogenes and mocking him, he told them, "Masters, say **what you [will]**, truly if I were not Alexander, I would be Diogenes."

[omitted material between lessons]

Narration and Discussion

Alexander was advised to introduce himself as a friendly, gentle ruler of the cities his father had conquered. Why did he reject this advice?

Why did Alexander say that he would choose to be Diogenes?

Older students: Part One of this lesson raises many questions about military aggression, including the treatment of civilians during wars. Could Alexander's destruction of Thebes be justified? If so, why did he later regret his actions?

Creative narration: Dramatize any part of this lesson.

Lesson Four

Introduction

In this lesson, Alexander fought successfully to cross the Granicus River and enter Persian territory. King Darius was not there himself; perhaps he thought it would be an easy matter for his troops (made up largely of mercenary soldiers) to push the Macedonians back.

Vocabulary

Delphi, to consult Apollo: the temple at Delphi contained the Oracle, believed to be a source of supernatural guidance. The prophecies were spoken through a woman called **"the priestess"** or "the nun."

importunity: persistence

prodigies: supernatural occurrences

presaging: foretelling

liberality: generosity

Diana (in Greek, Artemis): the goddess of the hunt and the moon

libations: offerings of wine

Achilles, Paris: characters in Homer's *Iliad*

sepulcher: tomb

to tarry Alexander…: to keep the Macedonians from crossing the river

phalanx: the classic Macedonian battle formation

People

Aristander: a soothsayer

Cleitus (Cleitus): "Cleitus the Black" saved Alexander's life in this battle, but was killed by him six years later during a drunken quarrel

Historic Occasions

June, 334 B.C.: Battle of the **Granicus River**

334 B.C.: The city of Sardis surrendered to Alexander

On the Map

After visiting Delphi, Alexander returned to Macedonia, gathered his forces, and headed east and then south, around the Aegean Sea, crossed the **Strait of Hellespont** (also called the Bosphorus); and finally arrived at the ancient site of Troy. The **Granicus River** was east of Troy.

Reading

Part One

Then he went to **Delphi, to consult Apollo** concerning the success of the war he had undertaken; and happening to come on one of the forbidden days, when it was esteemed improper to give any answer from the oracle, he sent messengers to desire **the priestess** to do her office; and when she refused, on the plea of a law to the contrary, he went up himself, and began to draw her by force into the temple, until tired and overcome with his **importunity:** "My son," said she, "thou art invincible." Alexander taking hold of what she spoke, declared he had received such an answer as he wished for, and that it was needless to consult the god any further.

Among other **prodigies** that attended the departure of his army, the image of Orpheus at Libethra, made of cypress-wood, was seen to sweat in great abundance, to the discouragement of many. But **Aristander** told him that, far from **presaging** any ill to him, it signified he should perform acts so important and glorious as would make the poets and musicians of future ages labour and sweat to describe and celebrate them.

His army, by the computation of those who make the smallest amount, consisted of thirty thousand foot and four thousand horse; and those who make the most of it speak but of forty-three thousand foot, and three thousand horse. Aristobulus says he had not a fund of above seventy talents for their pay; nor had he more than thirty days' provision, if we may believe Duris; Onesicritus tells us he was two hundred talents in debt.

Now, notwithstanding that he began this war with so small ability to maintain it, he would never take ship before he understood the state of his friends, to know what ability they had to go with him, and before he had given unto some, lands, and unto others, a town, and to others again, the revenue of some hamlet or harbour-town. Thus, by his bounty having in manner spent almost the revenues of the crown of Macedon, Perdiccas asked him: "My lord, what will you keep for yourself?" "Hope," said he. "Then," quoth Perdiccas again, "we will also have some part, since we go with you," and so he refused the revenue which the king had given him for his pension. Many others did also the like. But such as were contented to take his **liberality**, or would ask him anything, he gave them very frankly, and in such liberality he spent all the revenue he had.

With such vigorous resolutions, and his mind thus disposed, he passed the Hellespont, and at Troy sacrificed to **Diana** *[Dryden: Minerva]*, and honoured the memory of the heroes who were buried there, with solemn **libations**; especially **Achilles**, whose grave he anointed with oil, and with his friends, as the ancient custom is, ran naked about his **sepulcher**, and crowned it with garlands, declaring how happy he esteemed him, in having while he lived so faithful a friend, and when he was dead, so famous a poet to sing his praise.

When he had done, and went up and down the city to see all the monuments and notable things, someone asked him if he would like to see **Paris's** harp. He answered [that] he would prefer to see Achilles' harp, to which he used to sing the glories and great actions of brave men.

Part Two

In the meantime, Darius, king of Persia, having levied a great army, sent his captains and lieutenants **to tarry Alexander** at the **Granicus River**. There was Alexander to fight of necessity, it being the only bar to stop his entry into Asia. Moreover, his generals were afraid of the depth of this river, and of the height of the bank on the other side, which was very high and steep, and could not be won without fighting. And some said also, that he should have special care of the ancient regard of the month: because the kings of Macedon did never use to put their army into the field in the month of Dason *[or Daesius]*, which is June. "For that," said Alexander, "we will remedy soon: let them call it the second month, Artemisium, which is May." Furthermore, Parmenion was of opinion that he should not meddle the first day, because it was very late. Alexander made answer again, that the Hellespont would blush for shame if he were now afraid to pass over the river, since he had already come over an arm of the sea.

Thereupon he himself first entered the river with thirteen troops of horsemen, and marched forwards against an infinite number of arrows which the enemies shot at him as he was coming up the other bank, which was very high and steep, and worst of all, full of armed men and horsemen of the enemies: which stayed to receive him in battle array, thrusting his men down into the river, which was very deep, and ran so swift that it almost carried them down the stream: insomuch that men thought him more rash than wise, to lead his men with such danger.

However, he persisted obstinately to gain the passage, and at last with much ado making his way up the banks, which were extremely muddy and slippery, he had instantly to join in a mere confused hand-to-hand combat with the enemy, before he could draw up his men, who were still passing over, into any order. For the enemy pressed him with loud and warlike outcries; and charging horse against horse, plied with their lances; after they had broken and spent these, they fell to it with their swords. And Alexander, being easily known by his buckler, and a large plume of white feathers on each side of his helmet, was attacked on all sides, yet escaped wounding, though his [armour] was pierced by a javelin in one of the joinings.

Part Three

Thereupon Roesaces and Spithridates, two chief captains of the Persians, setting upon Alexander at once: he left the one, and riding straight to Roesaces, who was excellently armed, he gave him such a blow with his lance that he broke it in his hand, and straight drew out his sword. But so soon as they two had closed together, Spithridates coming at the side of him, raised himself upon his stirrups and gave Alexander with all his might such a blow of his head with a battle-axe, that he cut off the crest of his helmet, and one of the sides of his plume, and made such a gash that the edge of his battle-axe touched the very hair of his head. And as he was lifting up his hand to strike Alexander again, great **Cleitus**, preventing him, thrust him through with a spear; and at the very same instant, Roesaces also fell dead from his horse with a wound which Alexander gave him with his sword.

Now whilst the horsemen fought with such fury, the Macedonian **phalanx** passed the river, and the foot soldiers on each side advanced to fight. But the enemy hardly sustaining the first onset soon gave ground and fled, all but the mercenary Greeks, who drew together upon a hill, and craved mercy of Alexander. But Alexander setting upon them, more of will than discretion, had his horse killed under him, being thrust through the flank with a sword. This was not Bucephalus, but another horse he had. And this obstinacy of his to cut off these experienced desperate men cost him the lives of more of his own soldiers than all the battle before, besides, those who were wounded.

The Persians lost in this battle twenty thousand foot and two thousand five hundred horse. On Alexander's side, Aristobulus says there were not wanting above four-and-thirty, of whom nine were foot soldiers; and in memory of them he caused so many statues of brass, of Lysippus's making, to be erected. And because he would make the Grecians partakers of this victory, he sent unto the Athenians three hundred bucklers, which he had won at the battle, and upon the rest he put this honourable inscription: "Alexander the son of Philip, and the Grecians, excepting the Lacedaemonians, have won this spoil upon the barbarous Asians."

All the plate and purple garments, and other things of the same kind that he took from the Persians (except a very small quantity which he reserved for himself), he sent as a present to his mother.

Narration and Discussion

Why did Alexander take the words of the priestess as a prophecy?

"Alexander made answer again, that the Hellespont would blush for shame if he were now afraid to pass over the river..." What did he mean?

Creative narration: In a journal entry, or a letter to someone at home, describe the crossing of the Granicus.

For further thought: If you could see and touch some artifact from history (or from literature), what would you choose?

Lesson Five

Introduction

After their initial victory at the Battle of Granicus, the Macedonians seemed to have gained some respect from the Persian cities they passed through. Alexander and Darius both expected that they would soon fight face to face, but this was delayed by Alexander's illness in Cilicia.

Vocabulary

venture all: risk everything

by the Grecians: in this case, "Grecians" refers to the Macedonians

clear: conquer

the ancient Midas: a king of Phrygia, who allegedly turned everything he touched into gold

the knot: the Gordian Knot (see note before the reading)

levied: assembled

extreme pains and travail: exhaustion, overwork

People

Philip the Acarnanian: Alexander's personal physician

Historic Occasions

April-July, 333 B.C.: Alexander's visit to Gordium

September, 333 B.C.: Alexander arrived in Cilicia and became ill

On the Map

All the places named in this lesson are located in the region called **Asia**. Some of them will sound familiar to those who have read the Christian New Testament, especially the Book of Acts.

In Part One, the Macedonians' route after Granicus was south to **Sardis**, and then west to the **Mediterranean**, where they followed the coast around what is now southern Turkey, to the city of **Phaselis** on the coast of **Lycia**. In Part Two, they seem to have gone north (**Gordium** is more than halfway up to the **Black Sea**), and then looped around south again.

Phrygia: a kingdom of Asia

Xanthus (Xanthos) in Lycia: an ancient city, located in what is present-day Turkey, on the Mediterranean Sea

Cilicia: a region within the Persian empire, part of present-day Turkey

Phoenicia: a region east of the Mediterranean Sea, primarily located in present-day Lebanon

Pamphylia: a region between Lycia and Cilicia

Pisidia, Paphlagonia, Cappadocia: other regions of Asia

Susa: the capital city of the Persian Empire (in present-day Iran)

What was the Gordian Knot?

In **Phrygia**, once upon a time, it was decided that the next man to enter the city would become king. A farmer named Gordias came along driving an ox-cart, was therefore named king, and his now-unneeded cart was left there, tied up with an intricate knot. (Interestingly, Gordias is supposed to have been from Macedonia.) A

30

legend grew up that the one who undid the knot would rule Asia, and many would-be rulers tried but failed. Most tellers of the story say that Alexander simply cut the knot; but Plutarch offers an alternative version, saying that it was possible to undo the knot by removing the linchpin (a fastener) from the cart wheel.

"Cutting a Gordian knot" refers to a bold or unexpected solution to a difficult problem. But the famous preacher Charles Haddon Spurgeon, in a sermon titled "God's Providence," did not approve of Alexander's method, or (perhaps more) of his arrogance. He said, "God has many Gordian knots which wicked men may cut and which righteous men may try to unravel, but which God alone can untie."

Reading

Part One

This first victory brought such a sudden change amongst the barbarous people in Alexander's behalf, that the city itself of **Sardis**, the chief city of the empire of the barbarous people, or at the least through all the low countries and coasts upon the sea, they yielded straight unto him, excepting the cities of Halicarnassus and Miletus, which did still resist him: howbeit at length he took them by force.

When he had also conquered all thereabouts, he stood in doubt afterwards about what were best to do. Sometimes he had a marvellous desire wholly to follow Darius, wheresoever he were, and to **venture all** at a battle. Another time again, he thought it better first to occupy himself in conquering of these low countries, and to make himself strong with the money and riches he should find among them, that he might afterwards be the better able to follow him.

While he was thus deliberating what to do, it happened that a spring of water near the city of **Xanthus in Lycia**, of its own accord, swelled over its banks, and threw up a copper plate, upon the margin of which was engraved in ancient characters, that the time would come when the kingdom of the Persians should be destroyed **by the Grecians**. This did further so encourage Alexander that he made haste to **clear** all the sea coast, even as far as **Cilicia** and **Phoenicia**. But the wonderful good success he had, running alongst all the coast of **Pamphylia**, gave divers historiographers occasion to set forth his doings with admiration, saying that it was one of the wonders of the world that the fury of the sea, which unto all other was extremely rough, and many times would swell over the tops of the high rocks upon the cliffs, fell calm unto him.

[omission for length]

Part Two

Then he subdued the **Pisidians** *[omission]*; and conquered the Phrygians, at whose chief city, **Gordium**, which is said to be the seat of **the ancient Midas**, he saw the famous chariot fastened with cords made of the rind of the cornel-tree, which whosoever should untie, the inhabitants had a tradition that for him was reserved the empire of the world. Most authors tell the story that Alexander finding himself unable to untie **the knot**, the ends of which were secretly twisted round and folded up within it, cut it asunder with his sword. But Aristobulus tells us it was easy for him to undo it, by only pulling the pin out of the pole to which the yoke was tied, and afterwards drawing off the yoke itself from below.

From hence he advanced into **Paphlagonia and Cappadocia**, both which countries he soon reduced to obedience, and then hearing of the death of Memnon, the best commander Darius had upon the sea-coasts, and in whom was all their hope to trouble and withstand Alexander, he was the rather encouraged to carry the war into the upper provinces of Asia.

Part Three

Then did King Darius himself come against Alexander, having **levied** a great power at **Susa** of six hundred thousand fighting men; trusting to that multitude, and also to a dream, the which his wizards *[Dryden: the Persian soothsayers]* had expounded rather to flatter him than to tell him truly. Darius dreamed that he saw all the army of the Macedonians all on fire, and Alexander serving of him in the same attire that he himself wore when he was courier unto the late king his predecessor; and that when he came into the temple of Belus, he [Alexander] suddenly vanished from him. By this dream it plainly appeared that the gods did signify unto him that the Macedonians should have noble success in their doings, and that as he, from a courier's place, had risen to the throne, so Alexander should come to be master of Asia, and not long surviving his conquests, conclude his life with glory.

This furthermore made him bold also, when he saw that Alexander remained a good while in **Cilicia**, supposing it had been for that he was afraid of him. Howbeit it was by reason of a sickness he [Alexander] had, the which some say he got by **extreme pains and travail**, and others also, because he washed himself in the river of Cydnus, which was cold as ice. However, it happened, none of his physicians would venture to give him any remedies, they thought his case so desperate, and were so afraid of the suspicions and ill-will of the Macedonians if they should fail in the cure; till **Philip the Acarnanian**, seeing how critical his case was, but relying on his own well-known friendship for him, resolved to try the last efforts of his art, and rather hazard his own credit and life than suffer him to perish for want of physic, which he confidently administered to him, encouraging him to drink it boldly if he would quickly be whole, and go to the wars.

In the meantime, Parmenion wrote him [Alexander] a letter from the camp, advertising him that he should beware of Philip his physician, for he said that Philip was bribed and corrupted by Darius, with large promises of great riches that he would give him, along with his daughter in marriage, to kill his master.

Alexander when he had read this letter, laid it under his bed's head, and made none of his nearest familiars acquainted therewith. When the hour came that he should take his medicine, Philip came into his chamber, with some of the king's familiars, and brought a cup in his hand with the potion he should drink. Alexander then gave him the letter, and withal, cheerfully took the cup of him, showing no manner of fear or mistrust of anything. It was a wonderful thing and worth the sight, how one reading the letter, and the other drinking the medicine both at one instant, they looked one upon another, howbeit not both with like cheerful countenance.

For Alexander looked merrily upon him, plainly showing the trust he had in his physician Philip, and how much he loved him; and the physician also beheld Alexander, like a man perplexed and amazed, to be so falsely accused, and straight lifted up his hands to heaven, calling the gods to witness that he was innocent, and then came to Alexander's bedside, and prayed him to be of good cheer, and boldly to do as he would advise him.

The medicine, beginning to work, overcame the disease, and drove, for the time, to the lowest parts of his body, all his natural strength and powers: insomuch as his speech failed him, and he fell into such a weakness, and almost swooning, that his pulse did scant beat, and his senses were well near taken from him. However, in no long time, by Philip's means, his health and strength returned, and he showed himself in public to the Macedonians; for they would not be pacified, nor persuaded of his health, until they had seen him.

Narration and Discussion

Why did Alexander have so much success in conquering these regions of the Persian empire? To what did he give the credit?

How was Alexander's illness a Gordian knot for his physician?

Creative narration: The "wizards" (or "wise men") of Darius used his dream about Alexander to boost his confidence, by twisting its meaning. Plutarch's description of the dream, however, does not sound very affirming. How might it have been re-interpreted to sound more positive? This is a scene that could be written or acted out.

Creative narration: Both the cutting of the Gordian knot and the scene between Alexander and Philip would lend themselves to drama, art, or creative writing.

Lesson Six

Introduction

Plutarch sets the scene for the Battle of Issus, stating that the odds were against the Macedonians from the beginning: they were outnumbered and at a geographical disadvantage. Somehow, through good leadership and perhaps good luck, the Macedonians won an unexpected victory. King Darius escaped, but left everything behind, including his relatives and his bathtub.

Vocabulary

passes and defiles: narrow valleys or passages, usually through mountains

his horse: the Macedonian cavalry

four or five furlongs: four furlongs are half a mile (0.8 km)

sacking and spoiling: stealing all the valuables from a place, and usually destroying it in the process

vanquished: conquered

ewers: water jugs

sumptuous: rich, luxurious

People

Amyntas: Alexander had an officer named Amyntas, but this is someone else with the same name.

Antipater: see introductory notes

Historic Occasions

November, 333 B.C.: Battle of Issus

On the Map

Syria: Coele-Syria, a region which is part of present-day Syria and Lebanon

Issus is in the large gulf at the northeastern corner of the Mediterranean, between Antioch and Tarsus.

Cilician Gates: a pass through the mountains into that region

Reading

There was at this time in Darius's army a Macedonian refugee named Amyntas, one who was pretty well acquainted with Alexander's character. This man, when he saw Darius intended to fall upon the enemy in the **passes and defiles**, advised him earnestly to keep where he was, in the open and extensive plains, it being the advantage of a numerous army to have field-room enough when it engages with a lesser force. Darius, instead of taking his counsel, told him he was afraid the enemy would endeavour to run away, and so Alexander would escape out of his hands. Amyntas replied, "For that, O King, I pray you fear not: for I warrant you upon my life he will come to you, yea and is now onwards on his way coming towards you." All these persuasions of Amyntas could not turn Darius from making his camp to march towards Cilicia.

At the same time also, Alexander went towards **Syria** to meet with him. But it chanced one night, that the one of them missed of the other, and when day was come, they both returned back again.

Alexander, greatly pleased with this event, made all the haste he could to fight in the defiles; and Darius to recover his former ground, and draw his army out of so disadvantageous a place. For now he began to perceive his error in engaging himself too far in a country in which the sea, the mountains, and the River Pinarus running through the midst of it, would necessitate him to divide his forces, render **his horse** almost unserviceable, and only cover and support the weakness of the enemy.

But now, as Fortune gave Alexander the field as he would wish it to fight for his advantage, so could he tell excellently well how to set his men in battle array to win the victory. For being much inferior in numbers, so far from allowing himself to be outflanked, he did put out the right wing of his battle a great deal further than he did his left wing; and fighting himself in the left wing in the foremost ranks, he made all the barbarous people flee that stood before him: howbeit, he was hurt on his thigh with a blow of a sword. Chares writeth that Darius himself did hurt him, and that they fought together man to man *[Dryden: hand to hand]*. But in the account which he gave Antipater of the battle, though indeed he owns he was wounded in the thigh with a sword, though not dangerously, yet he takes no notice who it was that wounded him.

Thus, having won a famous victory, and slain above a hundred and ten thousand of his enemies, he could not yet take Darius, because he fled, having still **four or five furlongs'** advantage before him: howbeit he [Alexander] took his chariot of battle wherein he fought, and his bow also. Then he returned from the chase, and found the Macedonians **sacking and spoiling** all the rest of the camp of the barbarous people, where there was infinite riches (although they had left the most part of their carriage behind them in the city of Damascus, to come lighter to the battle); but they yet reserved for himself all King Darius' tent, which was full of a great number of rich movables, and of gold and silver. So, when he was come to the camp, putting off his armour, he entered into the bath and said, "Come on, let us go and wash off the sweat of the battle in Darius' own bath."

"Nay," replied one of his familiars again, "in Alexander's bath; for the goods of the **vanquished** are rightly the vanquisher's." When he came into the bath, and saw the basins and **ewers**, the boxes, and vials for perfumes, all of clean gold, excellently wrought, all the chamber perfumed passing sweetly, that it was like a paradise; then going out of his bath, and coming into his tent, seeing it so stately and large, his bed, the table, and supper, and all ready in such **sumptuous** sort, that it was wonderful, he turned him unto his familiars and said: "This was a king indeed, was he not, think ye?" *[Dryden: "This, it seems, is royalty."]*

Narration and Discussion

Why did Darius not take the advice of Amyntas, and fight in the open country where he was? Explain Amyntas' response.

What does this passage show about the character and leadership of Alexander?

Creative narration: You are a reporter on the scene after the Battle of Issus. Try to interview a variety of onlookers and participants. (This could be acted or written.) Another possibility: make a "Most Wanted" poster for King Darius, giving pertinent details.

Lesson Seven

Introduction

This lesson concludes the Battle of Issus, but it tells mainly about the generous and gallant aspects of Alexander's character.

Vocabulary

good hap: good fortune, luck

clemency: grace, generosity, mercy

pensions for their maintenance: financial allowances

usage: treatment

preceptor, governor: tutor and personal trainer

delicate or superfluous: self-indulgent, luxurious, unnecessary

nuptial solemnities: weddings

curious: careful

a temper of ostentation…: a bragging mood, showing off

a great advantage to ride him: an opportunity to mock him

base: demeaning, low

in a great strait: under a good deal of pressure

drachmas: a drachma was a silver coin

People

Leonnatus: a high-ranking Macedonian officer (not to be confused with **Leonidas**)

Princess Ada: Ada of Caria has an interesting history as a ruler. When Alexander entered her region of **Caria** (in present-day Turkey), Ada surrendered the fort she was holding, and in return he gave her command of the Siege of Halicarnassus.

Reading

As he was ready to go to his supper, word was brought to him that they were bringing unto him, amongst other ladies taken prisoners, King Darius' mother and his wife, and two unmarried daughters: who, having seen his chariot and bow, burst out into lamentable cries, and violent beating of themselves, thinking Darius had been slain. Alexander paused a good while and gave no answer, pitying more their misfortune than rejoicing at his own **good hap**. Then he presently sent **Leonnatus** unto them, to let them understand that Darius was alive, and that they should not need to be afraid of Alexander, for he did not fight with Darius, but for his kingdom only; and as for them, that they should have at his hands all that they had of Darius before, when he had his whole kingdom in his hands.

As these words pleased the captive ladies, so the deeds that followed made them find his **clemency** to be no less. For first he suffered them to bury as many of the Persian lords as they would, even of them that had been slain in the battle, and to take as much silks of the spoils, jewels, and ornaments, as they thought good to honour their funerals with; and also he did lessen no part of their honour, nor of the number of their officers and servants, nor of any jot of their estate which they had before, but did allow them also greater **pensions for their maintenance** than they had before. But the noblest and most royal part of their **usage** was that he treated these illustrious prisoners according to their virtue and character, not suffering them to hear, or receive, or so much as to apprehend anything that was unbecoming. So that they seemed rather lodged in some temple, or some holy virgin chambers, where they enjoyed their privacy sacred and uninterrupted, than in the camp of an enemy.

[omission: examples of Alexander's chastity]

[Alexander] was also no greedy gut, but temperate in eating, as he showed by many proofs: but chiefly in what he said unto **Princess Ada**, whom he adopted for his mother, and afterwards created queen of Caria. For when she, out of kindness, sent him every day many curious dishes and sweetmeats, and would have furnished him with some cooks and pastry-men, who were thought to have great skills, he told her he wanted none of them, his **preceptor, Leonidas,** having already given him the best, which were a night march to prepare for breakfast, and a moderate breakfast to create an appetite for supper. Leonidas also, he added, used to open and search the furniture of his chamber and his wardrobe, to see if his mother had left him anything that was **delicate or superfluous.**

Furthermore, he was less given to wine than men would have judged; that which gave people occasion to think so of him was, that when he had nothing else to do, he loved to sit long and talk, rather than drink, and over every cup hold a long conversation. For when his affairs called upon him, he would not be detained, as other generals often were, either by wine, or sleep, **nuptial solemnities**, spectacles, or any other diversion whatsoever; a convincing argument of which is, that in the short time he lived, he accomplished so many and so great actions.

When he had leisure, after he was up in the morning, first of all he would do sacrifice to the gods, and then would go to dinner, passing away all the rest of the day in hunting, writing something, taking up some quarrel between soldiers, or else in studying. If he went on any journey of no hasty business, he would exercise himself by the way as he went, shooting in his bow, or learning to get up or out of his chariot suddenly, as it ran. Oftentimes also for his pastime he would hunt the fox or catch birds, as appeareth in his book of remembrances for every day. Then when he came to his lodging, he would enter into his bath, and rub and anoint himself, and would ask his bakers and chief cooks if his supper were ready. He would ever sup late, and he was very **curious** to see that every man at his board were alike served, and he would sit long at the table, because he ever loved to talk, as we have told you before. And then, though otherwise no prince's conversation was ever so agreeable, he would fall into **a temper of ostentation and soldierly boasting**, which gave his flatterers a great advantage to **ride** him, and made his better friends very uneasy. For though they thought it too **base** to strive who should flatter him most, yet they found it hazardous not to do it; so that between the shame and the danger, they were **in a great strait** how to behave themselves. After supper, he would wash himself again, and sleep until noon the next day following, and oftentimes all day long.

He was so very temperate in his eating that when any rare fish or fruits were sent him, he would distribute them among his friends, and often reserve nothing for himself. His table notwithstanding was always very honourably served, and he did still increase his fare, as he did enlarge his conquests, till it came to the sum of ten thousand **drachmas** a day. But there he stayed, and would not exceed that sum, and moreover commanded all men that would feast him, that they should not spend above that sum.

Narration and Discussion

How did Alexander treat the female relatives of King Darius? What does this show about his character?

In what ways did Alexander show moderation in his personal life? How did those habits allow him to get a lot done?

Creative narration: In a creative way, tell about Alexander's teacher Leonidas. (Somewhat anachronistic possibilities might include Alexander flipping through his childhood photo album.)

For further thought: In 332 B.C., Alexander "conquered" Palestine while on his way to Egypt; and the historian Josephus wrote (much later) that Alexander visited the temple in Jerusalem and that a priest showed him prophecies—possibly about himself—in the Book of Daniel. Whether or not that story is true, it is not impossible that Alexander read some Old Testament writings along with his other books. Choose a passage from the Book of Proverbs, or Ecclesiastes, and consider what impact it might have had on this young ruler.

Lesson Eight

Introduction

Alexander never seemed to stop moving and conquering. His army bulldozed southward through many ancient strongholds, eventually taking even the stubborn city of Tyre.

Vocabulary

gallantry: bravery

barbarous: in this case, the luxurious Persian lifestyle

necessary to assure himself of the seacoast: he needed to take control of the ports along the coast of the Mediterranean

bulwarks and divers engines of battery: war machines and weapons

benighted: forced to stop for the night

firebrand: torch, or blazing stick of wood from the fire

entrails: innards

prognosticate: prophesy

frankincense, myrrh: aromatic (fragrant) gum resins, burned as incense

People

Lysimachus: see introductory notes

Phoenix, Achilles' guardian: Phoenix went with Achilles to the Trojan war, in Homer's *Iliad*

Historic Occasions

332 B.C.: Alexander conquered Tyre in Phoenicia, then Syria

On the Map

Alexander followed the eastern coast of the Mediterranean, through **Phoenicia**, and besieged **Tyre**. The Macedonians then marched through **Syria** (see map notes for **Lesson Six**) and Palestine (including the city of **Gaza**).

Damascus: the capital city of Syria

Cyprus: the third-largest island in the Mediterranean

Mount Antilibanus: mountains between Syria and Lebanon

Reading

Part One

After the Battle of Issus [**Lesson Six**], Alexander sent to **Damascus** to seize upon the money and baggage, the wives and children of the Persians, of which spoil the Thessalian horsemen had the greatest share; for he had taken particular notice of their **gallantry** in the fight, and sent them thither on purpose to make their reward suitable to their courage; and so were the rest of his army also well stored with money. There the Macedonians having tasted first of the gold, silver, women, and **barbarous** life: as dogs by scent do follow the track of beasts, even so were they greedy to follow after the goods of the Persians. But Alexander, before he proceeded any further, thought it **necessary to assure himself of the seacoast**. Those who governed in **Cyprus** put that island into his possession, and Phoenicia, **the city of Tyre** only excepted, was surrendered to him. That city he besieged seven months together by land, with great **bulwarks and divers engines of battery**, and by sea, with two hundred galleys.

[omission for length: Alexander's dreams of Hercules and mythical beasts]

Continuing this siege, he went to make war with the Arabians that dwell upon **Mount Antilibanus**, in which he hazarded his life extremely to [save] his master **Lysimachus**, who would needs go along with him, declaring that he was neither "older nor inferior in courage to **Phoenix**," Achilles' guardian. For when they came at the foot of the mountain, they left their horses, and went up afoot: and Alexander was of so courteous a nature, that he would not leave his tutor Lysimachus behind him (who was so weary that he could go no further); but because it was dark night, and for that the enemies were not far from them, he came behind to encourage his tutor, and in manner to carry him. By this means, unawares, he was far from his army with very few men about him, and **benighted** besides: moreover, it was very cold, and the way was very ill.

At the length, perceiving divers fires which the enemies had made, some in one place, and some in another, trusting to his valiantness, having always provided remedy in extremity when the Macedonians were distressed, himself ever putting to his own hand: he ran unto them that had made the fires next him, and killing two of the barbarous people that lay by the fireside, he snatched away a **firebrand**, and ran with it to his own men, who made a great fire. At this the barbarous people were so afraid, that they ran their way as fast as they could. Others also thinking to come and set upon him, he slew them every man, and so lay there that night, himself and his men without danger. Thus Chares reporteth this matter.

Part Two

Now for the siege of Tyre, that fell out thus. Alexander caused the most part of his army to take rest, being overharried and wearied with so many battles as they had fought: and sent a few of his men only to give assault unto the city, to keep the Tyrians occupied, that they should take no rest. One day the soothsayer Aristander sacrificing unto the gods, having considered of the signs of the **entrails** of the beasts, did assure them that were present, that the city should be taken by the latter end of the month. Everybody laughed to hear him: for that day was the very last day of the month. Alexander seeing him amazed, as one that could not tell what to say to it, seeking ever to bring those tokens to effect which the soothsayers did **prognosticate**: he gave orders that they should not count it as the thirtieth, but as the twenty-third of the month. He made the trumpet sound the alarm, and give a hotter assault to the wall than he had thought to have done before. They fought valiantly on both sides, insomuch as they that were left in the camp could not keep in but must needs run to the assault to help their companions. The Tyrians seeing the assault so hot on every side, their hearts began to fail them, and by this means was the city taken the selfsame day.

[short omission]

Part Three

Alexander sent great presents of spoils which he won at the sack of **Gaza** unto his mother Olympias, his stepmother Cleopatra, and divers others of his friends. Among other things, he sent unto Leonidas, his governor [**Lesson Seven**], five hundred talents' weight of **frankincense** and a hundred talents' weight of **myrrh**, remembering the hope he put him into when he was a child. For, as Alexander was one day sacrificing unto the gods, he took both his hands full of frankincense to cast into the fire, to make a perfume thereof. When Leonidas saw him, he said thus unto him: "When thou hast conquered the country where these sweet things grow, then be liberal of thy perfume: but now, spare that little thou hast at this present." Alexander calling to mind at that time his admonition, wrote unto him in this sort: "We do send thee plenty of frankincense and myrrh, because thou shouldst no more be a miser unto the gods."

Narration and Discussion

Alexander's world was full of prophecies, dreams, and sacrifices to gods. At the same time, his methods of warfare seem to have been extremely practical: war engines, sieges, and, when necessary, stealing fire and stabbing those he believed to be enemies. Does Alexander seem to have put more trust in the supernatural, or in his own strength?

How did Alexander's gift to his old tutor show a sense of humour?

Creative narration: Dramatize the story of changing the calendar. (You might tell it from the perspective of someone who has to deal with several days suddenly added to their month.)

Lesson Nine

Introduction

Alexander marked his time in Egypt first by laying out plans for the city of Alexandria, and then by taking an arduous pilgrimage through the desert to the temple of Jupiter Ammon.

Vocabulary

casket: box, chest

a great city: Alexandria

these verses: these are lines from Homer's *Odyssey*

mole: a stone causeway or raised road

isthmus: a narrow strip of land

the charge of the building: Alexander remained in Egypt for only a few months and never saw more than the foundations of the city.

seconded: assisted

element: sky, heavens

blaspheme: speak irreverently about sacred things

it went for current: the rumour went around

divine generation: being born of gods

Historic Occasions

331? B.C.: the founding of Alexandria. Some sources give the date as 332, or even 334.

On the Map

The Macedonians made a long, looping journey through the northern part of Egypt, stopping along the way to establish Alexandria on the Mediterranean coast. This detour was due to Alexander's wish to visit the temple of **Jupiter Ammon,** or Zeus Ammon. Ammon was the Greek name for the Egyptian god Aman; they must have found it fitting, because "ammos" is the Greek word for "sand."

Pharos: a small island on the western edge of the Nile Delta

Reading

Part One

Among the treasures and other booty that was taken from Darius, there was a very precious **casket**, which, being brought to Alexander for a great rarity, he asked those about him what they thought fittest to be laid up in it. Some said one thing, some said another thing: but he said, he would put Homer's *Iliad* into it, as the worthiest thing. This is confirmed by the best historiographers; and if what those of Alexandria tell us, relying upon the authority of Heraclides, be true, then it appeareth that he did profit himself much by Homer in this journey.

For it is reported that when he had conquered Egypt, he determined to build **a great city**, and to replenish it with a great number of Grecians, and to call it after his name. But as he was about to enclose a certain ground, which he had chosen by the advice of his engineers and workmasters: the night before he had a marvellous dream, that he saw an old man standing before him, full of white hairs, with an honourable presence, who coming towards him said **these verses**:

"An island lies, where loud the billows roar,

Pharos, they call it, on the Egyptian shore."

Alexander upon this immediately rose up and went to **Pharos**, which at that time was an island lying a little above the Canobic mouth of the river Nile, though it has now been joined to the mainland by a **mole**. As soon as he saw the commodious situation of the place, it being a long neck of land, stretching like an **isthmus** between large lagoons and shallow waters on one side and the sea on the other, the latter at the end of it making a spacious harbour, he said, "Homer, besides his other excellences, was a very good architect," and he ordered the plan of a city to be drawn out answerable to the place. To do which, for want of chalk, the soil being black, they laid out their lines with flour [Dryden: *meal*], taking in a pretty large compass of ground in a semi-circular figure, and drawing into the inside of the circumference equal straight lines from each end, thus giving it something of the form of a cloak or cape.

While he was pleasing himself with his design, on a sudden an infinite number of great birds of several kinds, rising like a black cloud out of the river and the lake, devoured every morsel of the flour that had been used in setting out the lines; at which omen even Alexander himself was troubled. Notwithstanding, his soothsayers bade him not be discouraged, for they told him it was a sign that he should build a city there, so plentiful of all things, that he should maintain all sorts of people. Then he commanded them unto whom he had given **the charge of the building**, that they should go forward with their work; and he himself, in the meantime, took his journey to go visit the temple of **Jupiter Ammon**.

Part Two

This was a long and painful, and, in two respects, a dangerous journey; first, if they should lose their provision of water, as for several days none could be obtained; and, secondly, if a violent south wind should rise upon them, while they were travelling through the wide extent of deep sands, as it is said to have done when Cambyses led his army that way, blowing the sand together in heaps, and raising, as it were, the whole desert like a sea upon them, till fifty thousand were swallowed up and destroyed by it.

All these difficulties were weighed and represented to him; but Alexander was not easily to be diverted from anything he was bent upon. For Fortune having hitherto **seconded** him in his designs, made him resolute and firm in his opinions, and the boldness of his temper raised a sort of passion in him for surmounting difficulties, as if it were not enough to be always victorious in the field, unless places and seasons and nature herself submitted to him.

In that journey, the relief and assistance the gods afforded him in his distresses were more remarkable, and obtained greater belief than the oracles he received afterwards, which, however, were valued and credited the more on account of those occurrences. First of all, the wonderful water and great showers that fell from the **element** did keep him from fear of the first danger, and did quench their thirst, and moistened the dryness of the sand in such sort, that there came a sweet fresh air from it. Furthermore, when the marks were hidden from the guides to show them the way, and they wandered up and down, they could not tell where: there came crows unto them that did guide them, flying before them: flying fast when they saw them follow them, and staying for them when they were behind. But Callisthenes writeth a greater wonder than this: that in the nighttime, with the very noise of the crows, they brought them again into the right way those which had lost their way.

Thus, Alexander in the end having passed through this wilderness, he came unto the temple he sought for: where the prophet or chief priest saluted him from the god Ammon, as from his father. Then Alexander asked him, if any of the murderers that had killed his father were left alive. The priest answered him, and bade him take heed he did not **blaspheme**, for his father was no mortal man. Then Alexander *[brief omission]* asked him if the murderers that had conspired the death of Philip his father were all punished.

After that he asked him, touching his kingdom, if he would grant him to be king over all the world. The god answered him by the mouth of his prophet, he should: and that the death of Philip was fully revenged. Then did Alexander offer great presents unto the god, and he gave much money to the priests and ministers of the temple. This is that which the most part of writers do declare, touching Alexander's demand, and the oracles given him. Yet did Alexander himself write unto his mother that he had secret oracles from the god, which he would only impart unto her at his return into Macedon.

Others say that the priest, desirous as a piece of courtesy to address him in Greek by saying "O Paidion" (dear son), by a slip in pronunciation ended with the "s" instead of the "n," and said "O Paidios" (son of Jupiter), which mistake Alexander was well enough pleased with; and **it went for current** that the oracle had called him so.

Part Three (optional)

It is said also, that he heard Psammon the philosopher in Egypt, and that he liked his words very well, when he said that God was king of all mortal men: "For," (quoth he), "he that commandeth all things must needs be God." But Alexander himself spoke better, and like a philosopher, when he said that God generally was father to all mortal men, but that particularly he did elect the best sort for himself. To conclude, he showed himself more arrogant unto the barbarous people, and made as though he certainly believed that he had been begotten of some god; but unto the Grecians he spoke more modestly of **divine generation.**

For in a letter he wrote unto the Athenians touching the city of Samos, he said: "I gave ye not that noble free city, but it was given you, at that time, by him whom they called my lord and father": meaning Philip. Afterwards also, being stricken with an arrow and feeling great pain of it: "My friends," said he, "This blood which is spilt is man's blood, and not as Homer said: 'No such as from the immortal gods doth flow.'"

[short omission]

Narration and Discussion

How did Alexander "profit himself much by Homer in this journey?"

How did the soothsayers reassure Alexander after the birds ate up his plans for the city?

For older students: Plutarch says, "But Alexander himself spoke better, and like a philosopher, when he said that God generally was father to all mortal men, but that particularly he did elect the best sort for himself." Compare this with Christian beliefs (e.g. John 3:16).

For further thought: Was Alexander's strength and success due to his own skills, to the favouring of "Fortune," or was there something else behind it?

Lesson Ten

Introduction

This lesson moves from the imagined tragedies at a drama contest to the real grief of Darius at the loss of his queen. Surprisingly, this gave Darius less anger at Alexander (who had caused their separation), but rather more respect for him. However, since Alexander had rejected Darius' negotiations for a peaceful sharing of the Persian empire, the only possible response was a final battle.

Vocabulary

tragedies: theatrical performances

equipage: equipment, stage sets

chorus: in Greek theater, a group of actors who commented on the action of the play, usually with song and dance

satisfy the penalty: pay the fine

ten talents: a very large sum of money

ten thousand talents: an incredibly large sum of money

amity and alliance: friendship and co-operation

without dissimulation: without any pretense

eunuch: a particular type of male servant

travail of child: childbirth

On the Map

Alexander ended his Egyptian journey, retraced his route back to Tyre, headed east through Damascus, and eventually crossed the **Euphrates River.**

Reading

Part One

At his return out of Egypt into Phoenicia, he sacrificed and made solemn processions, to which were added shows of lyric dances and

tragedies, remarkable not merely for the splendour of the **equipage** and decorations, but for the competition among those who exhibited them. For the kings of Cyprus were here the exhibitors, just in the same manner as at Athens those who are chosen by lot out of the tribes. And, indeed, they [tried to outdo] each other; especially Nicocreon, king of Salamis, and Pasicrates of Soli, who furnished the **chorus,** and defrayed the expenses of the two most celebrated actors, Athenodorus and Thessalus, the former performing for Pasicrates, and the latter for Nicocrean. Thessalus was most favoured by Alexander, though it did not appear till Athenodorus was declared victor by the plurality of votes. For when he went from the plays, he told them he did like the judges' opinion well; notwithstanding, he would have been contented to have given the one half of his realm not to have seen Thessalus overcome. However, when he understood Athenodorus was fined by the Athenians for being absent at the festivals of Bacchus, though he refused his request that he would write a letter in his behalf, he gave him a sufficient sum to **satisfy the penalty.** Also, when Lycon of Scarphia, an excellent stage player, had pleased Alexander well and did slip in a verse in his comedy in which he begged for a present of **ten talents:** Alexander, laughing at it, gave it to him.

Part Two

Darius at that time wrote unto Alexander, and unto certain of his friends also, to pray him to take **ten thousand talents** for the ransom of all those prisoners he had in his hands, offering him in exchange for his **amity and alliance** all the countries on this side of the river Euphrates, and one of his daughters also in marriage, that from thenceforth he might be his kinsman and friend. These propositions he communicated to his friends, and when Parmenion told him that, for his part, if he were Alexander, he should readily embrace them, "So would I indeed," said Alexander, "if I were Parmenion." Accordingly, his answer to Darius was, that if he would come and yield himself up into his power he would treat him with all possible kindness; if not, he was resolved immediately go himself and seek him. But the death of Darius's wife in childbirth made him soon after regret one part of this answer; and he showed evident marks of grief at being thus deprived of a further opportunity of exercising his courtesy and clemency. This notwithstanding, he gave her body honourable burial, sparing for no cost.

Among the **eunuchs** who waited in the queen's chamber and were taken prisoners with the women, there was one Tireus, who, getting out of the camp, fled away on horseback to Darius, to inform him of his wife's death. Then Darius beating of his head, and weeping bitterly, cried out aloud: "Oh gods! what wretched hap have the Persians! that have not only had the wife and sister of their king taken prisoners even in his lifetime, but now that she is dead also in **travail of child**, she hath been deprived of princely burial!"

Then spoke the eunuch to him, and said:

> "For her burial, most gracious King, and for all due
> honour that might be wished her, Persia hath no
> cause to complain of her hard fortune. For neither
> did Queen Statira your wife, whilst she lived
> prisoner, nor your mother nor daughters, want any
> part or jot of their honour they were wont to have
> before, saving only to see the light of your honour,
> the which the god Oromasdes will grant to restore
> again (if it be his will) unto your Majesty: neither
> was there any honour wanting at her death (to set
> forth her stately funerals) that might be gotten, but
> more was lamented also with the tears of your
> enemies. For Alexander is as merciful in victory as
> he is valiant in battle."

[omission]

Then Darius coming out among his friends again, holding up his hands unto the heavens, made this prayer unto the gods:

> "O heavenly gods, creators of men, and protectors
> of kings and realms: First, I beseech you, grant me
> that restoring the Persians again to their former
> good state, I may leave the realm unto my
> successors, with that glory and fame I received it of
> my predecessors; that obtaining victory, I may use
> Alexander with that great honour and courtesy
> which he hath in my misery shown unto those I
> loved best in the world. Or otherwise, if the time

appointed be come that the kingdom of Persia must needs have end, either through divine revenge, or by natural change of earthly things: then good gods yet grant that none but Alexander after me may sit in Cyrus' throne."

Divers writers do agree that these things came even thus to pass.

Narration and Discussion

Why did the Macedonians stage dramatic contests and other "pastimes" at that time?

Why did Alexander reject the offers from King Darius?

Why was Tireus so anxious to tell Darius that his wife had received proper treatment and a royal funeral? Might he not instead have wished to cast a negative light on Alexander?

For older students and further thought: How did Darius' prayer show magnanimity?

Lesson Eleven

Introduction

Plutarch leads up to the Battle of Gaugamela by describing some playfighting which got out of hand, but which also foreshadowed Alexander's victory.

Vocabulary

> **The servants who followed the camp:** this is Dryden's phrase. North translates it "the slaves of his army."

> **heated with contention:** hot-headed and ready to fight

> **leave:** permission

he confided in: he had confidence in

worsted: beaten

munition: weapons

out of their battle: out of formation

carriage: weapons and other supplies

girt close about him: close-fitting

exhortations: speeches

People

Philotas, Parmenion: see introductory notes

Historic Occasions

October, 331 B.C.: Battle of **Gaugamela**

On the Map

Alexander continued eastward, crossing the Euphrates, heading somewhat north to cross the Tigris (another major river), following the Tigris for a distance, and ending up at the site of the battle (in today's northern Iraq).

mountains of the Gordyaeans: the Corduene region, in what is now eastern Turkey

Reading

Part One

Now Alexander having conquered all Asia this side of the Euphrates, he went to meet with Darius, who came down with ten hundred thousand fighting men *[Dryden: a million of men]*. In his march a very ridiculous passage happened. **The servants who followed the camp,** for sport's sake, divided themselves into two parties, and named the commander of one of them "Alexander," and the other "Darius." At first they only pelted one another with clods of earth, but presently took to their fists, and at last, **heated with contention**, they fought in good earnest with stones and clubs, so that they had much ado to part them; till Alexander, upon hearing of it, ordered the two captains to decide the quarrel by single combat, and armed him who bore his name himself, while **Philotas** did the same to him who represented Darius. All the army thereupon was gathered together to see this combat between them, as a thing that did betoken good or ill luck to some. The fight was sharp between them, but in the end, he that was called "Alexander" overcame the other. Alexander, to reward him, gave him twelve villages, with **leave** to wear the Persian dress. Thus it is written by Eratosthenes.

Part Two

The great battle that [the real] Alexander fought with Darius, was not (as many writers report) at Arbela, but at **Gaugamela**, which signifies in the Persian tongue, "the house of the camel." For some one of the ancient kings of Persia that had escaped from the hands of his enemies, fleeing upon a swift camel, in gratitude to his beast, settled him at this place, with an allowance of certain villages and rents for his maintenance.

There fell out at that time an eclipse of the moon, in the month called *Boedromion* (now August), about the time that the Feast of the Mysteries was celebrated at Athens. The eleventh night after that, both their armies being in sight of the other, Darius kept his men in battle array, and went himself by torchlight, viewing his bands and companies. Alexander, on the other side, whilst his Macedonian soldiers slept, was before his tent with Aristander the soothsayer; and made certain secret ceremonies and sacrifices unto Apollo *[Dryden: the god Fear]*.

The oldest captains of the Macedonians, specially **Parmenion**, seeing all the valley betwixt the river of Niphates, and the **mountains of the Gordyaeans**, all on a bright light with the fires of the barbarous people, and hearing a dreadful noise as of a confused multitude of people that filled their camp with the sound thereof: they were amazed, and concluded that in one day it was in manner impossible to fight a battle with such an incredible multitude of people.

Thereupon they went unto Alexander after he had ended his ceremonies, and did counsel him to give battle by night, because the darkness thereof should help to keep all fear from his men, which the sight of their enemies would bring them into. To this he gave them the celebrated answer, "I will not steal a victory." Some at the time thought it a boyish and inconsiderate speech, as if he played with danger. Others, however, regarded it as evidence that **he confided in** his present condition, and acted on a true judgment of the future, not wishing to leave Darius, in case he were **worsted**, the pretext of trying his fortune again, which he might suppose himself to have, if he could impute his overthrow to the disadvantage of the night, as he did before to the mountains, the narrow passages, and the sea. "For," said he, "Darius will never leave to make wars with us for lack of men, nor **munition**, having so large a realm as he hath, and such a world of people besides; but then he will no more hazard battle, when his heart is done, and all hope taken from him, and that he seeth his army at noonday overthrown by plain battle."

After his captains were gone from him, he went into his tent, and laid him down to sleep, and slept all that night more soundly than he was wont to do before: insomuch as the lords and princes of his camp coming to wait upon him at his uprising, marvelled when they found him so sound asleep, and therefore of themselves they commanded the soldiers to eat. Afterwards, perceiving that time came fast upon them, Parmenion went into Alexander's chamber, and coming to his bedside, called him twice or thrice by his name, till at the last he waked him and asked him how it chanced that he slept so long, like one that had already overcome, and that did not think he should fight as great and dangerous a battle as ever he did in his life. "And are we not so, indeed," replied Alexander, smiling, "since we are at last relieved from the trouble of wandering in pursuit of Darius through a wide and wasted country, hoping in vain that he would fight us?"

Part Three

Now Alexander did not only show himself before the battle, but even at the very instant of battle, a noble man of courage and of great judgment. For Parmenion leading the left wing of his battle, the men of arms of the Bactrians gave such a fierce onset upon the Macedonians that they made them give back: and Mazeus also, King Darius' lieutenant, sent certain troops of horsemen **out of their battle** to give charge upon them that were left in the camp to guard the baggage.

This so disturbed Parmenion that he sent messengers to acquaint Alexander that the camp and baggage would be all lost, unless he immediately relieved the rear by a considerable reinforcement drawn out of the front. When this news came to Alexander from Parmenion, he had already given the signal of battle unto his men to give charge. Whereupon he answered the messenger that brought him these news, that he should tell Parmenion he was a madman and out of his wits, not remembering that if they won the battle, they should not only save their own **carriage**, but also win the carriage of their enemies: and if it were their chance to lose it, then that they should not need to care for their carriage, nor for their slaves, but only to think to die honourably, valiantly fighting for his life.

Having sent this message unto Parmenion, he put on his helmet. The rest of his armour he had put on before in his tent, which were a coat of the Sicilian make, **girt close about him**, and over that a breast-piece of thickly quilted linen, which was taken among other [spoils] at the Battle of Issus. His iron headpiece was as bright as silver, made by Theophilus the armourer: his collar *[Dryden: gorget]* was of the same metal, all set full of precious stones; and he had a sword by his side, marvellous light, and of excellent temper, which the king of the Citieians had given him, using commonly to fight with his sword at any set battle. His coat armour was marvellous rich, and of sumptuous workmanship, far above all the rest he wore. It was of the workmanship of Hellicon, which the Rhodians gave him for a present, and this he commonly wore when he went to battle.

Now when he did set his men in battle array, or made any oration unto them, or did ride alongst the bands to take view of them: he always used to ride upon another horse to spare Bucephalus, because he was then somewhat old: notwithstanding, when he meant indeed to fight, then Bucephalus was brought unto him, and as soon as he was gotten up on his back, the trumpet sounded, and he gave charge.

Then, after he had made long **exhortations** to encourage the men of arms of the Thessalians, and the other Grecians also, and when they had all promised him they would stick to him like men, and prayed him to lead them, and give charge upon the enemies: he took his lance in his left hand, and holding up his right hand unto heaven, besought the gods (as Callisthenes writeth) that if it were true he was begotten of Jupiter, that it would please them that day to help him, and to encourage the Grecians. The soothsayer Aristander was then a-horseback [near] Alexander, appareled all in white, and a crown of gold on his head; [he] showed Alexander, when he made his prayer, an eagle flying over his head and pointing directly towards his enemies. This marvellously encouraged all the army that saw it, and with this joy, the men of arms of Alexander's side, encouraging one another, did set spurs to their horse to charge upon the enemies.

Narration and Discussion

How did the sham battles between "Alexander" and "Darius" get out of hand? How were they resolved?

"I will not steal a victory." What did Alexander mean?

Why was Alexander able to sleep so well the night before the battle?

For those interested in military strategy: There are various opinions about whether Alexander meant to trick Darius by taking an unexpected northern route to Gaugamela, or whether he chose it to avoid the heat and have better access to food. There are also questions about why that part of the Tigris was undefended, and the Macedonians were able to cross it without trouble. Was Darius merely careless, or was he leading Alexander into a trap by choosing a battlefield that (he thought) suited his strengths?

Lesson Twelve

Introduction

This lesson ends the story of the Battle of Gaugamela, which marked

Alexander's victory over the Persian Empire. It also introduces his new status as "King of Asia."

Vocabulary

dispersed themselves: broke ranks and ran away

let, hinder: get in the way or prevent

made no countenance to flee: seemed to have no intention of fleeing

Somewhat there was in it: There was some truth in it

continue the execution: continue what they were doing

laudable: praiseworthy

naphtha, bitumen: Bitumen is asphalt, and it was used in the ancient world for many purposes including mummification. The naphtha shown to Alexander may have been a crude oil version of the thicker, stickier bitumen. North spells it "naptha," but as that now commonly refers to mineral spirits, I have used "naphtha."

unctuous: oily

peradventure: perhaps

ready coin: metals already made into coins

tincture: dye mixture

People

Phayllos the wrestler: Phayllos of Croton, who commanded a ship at the Battle of Salamis in 480 B.C.

Harpalus: see introductory notes

On the Map

After the Battle of Gaugamela, Alexander headed south to Babylon, and east to Susa. He marched a long way to the northwest to arrive at

Ecbatana; then, it appears, he returned south.

Reading

Part One

The battle [formation] of the footmen of the Persians began to give way a little, and before the foremost could come to give them charge, the barbarous people turned their backs, and fled. The chase was great, Alexander driving them that fled upon the midst of their own [ranks], where Darius himself was in person. He spied him afar off over the foremost ranks, in the midst of his life-guard, being a goodly tall prince, standing in a chariot of war, compassed in round with great troops of horsemen, all set in goodly ordinance to receive the enemy. But when they saw Alexander at hand with so grim a look, chasing them that fled through those that yet kept their ranks: there fell such a fear among them, that the most part **dispersed themselves**. Notwithstanding, the best and most valiantest men fought it out to the death before their king, and falling dead one upon another, they did **let** them that the enemies could not so well follow Darius. For they, lying one by another on the ground, drawing on to the last gasp, did yet take both men and horses by the legs to **hinder** them.

Darius then seeing nothing but terror and destruction before his eyes, and that the bands which he had set before him for safeguard came back upon him so as he could not devise how to turn his chariot forward nor backward, the wheels were so hindered and stayed with the heaps of dead bodies, and that the horses also being set upon and almost hidden in this conflict, fell to leaping and plunging for fear, so that the charioteers could no longer guide nor drive them: he got up upon a mare that lately had foaled, and so saved himself, fleeing upon her. And yet he would not have thus escaped, had not Parmenion once again sent unto Alexander to pray him to come and aid him: because there was yet a great squadron of Persians that **made no countenance to flee. Somewhat there was in it**, that they accused Parmenion that day to have dealt but slackly and cowardly, either because his age had taken his courage from him, or else for that he envied Alexander's greatness and prosperity, who against his [Parmenion's] will became over-great, as Callisthenes said. Alexander, though he was not a little vexed to be so recalled and hindered from pursuing his victory, yet concealed the true reason from his men, and causing a retreat to be sounded, as if it were too late to **continue the execution** any longer, marched back towards the place of danger. Notwithstanding, news came to him by the way that in that place also they had given the enemies the overthrow, and that they fled every way for life.

The battle being thus over, seemed to put a period to the Persian empire; and Alexander, who was now proclaimed King of Asia, returned thanks to the gods in magnificent sacrifices, and rewarded his friends and followers with great sums of money, and places, and governments of provinces.

Furthermore, to show his liberality also unto the Grecians, he wrote unto them that he would have all tyrannies suppressed throughout all Greece, and that all the Grecians should live at liberty under their own laws. Particularly also he wrote unto the Plataeians, that he would re-edify their city again, because their predecessors in time past, had given their country unto the Grecians, to fight against the barbarous people for the defense of the common liberty of all Greece.

He sent also into, Italy unto the Crotonians, part of the spoil, to honour **Phayllos the wrestler** who in the time of the wars with the Medes (when all the Grecians that dwelt in Italy had forsaken their natural countrymen of Greece itself, because they thought they could not otherwise escape), went with a ship of his unto Salamis, which he armed and set forth at his own charges, because he would be at the battle and partake also of the common danger with the Grecians. So affectionate was Alexander to all kinds of virtue, and so desirous to preserve the memory of **laudable** actions.

Then Alexander marching with his army into the country of Babylon, they all yielded straight unto him.

Part Two (optional)

In **Ecbatana** he was much surprised at the sight of the place where fire issues in a continuous stream, like a spring of water, out of a cleft in the earth, and the stream of **naphtha**, which, not far from this spot, flows out so abundantly as to form a sort of lake. This naphtha, in other respects resembling **bitumen**, is so subject to take fire, that before it touches the flame it will kindle at the very light that surrounds it, and often inflame the intermediate air also. The barbarous people of that country, being desirous to show Alexander the nature of that naphtha, scattered the street that led to his lodging with some of it. Then the day being shut in, they fired it at one of the ends, and the first drops taking fire, in the twinkling of an eye, all the rest from one end of the street to the other was of a flame, and though it was dark and within night, lightened all the place thereabout.

[Omission: a sadistic experiment with naphtha]

The manner, however, of the production of naphtha admits of a diversity of opinion…of whether this liquid substance that feeds the flame does not rather proceed from a soil that is **unctuous** and productive of fire, as that of the province of Babylon is, where the ground is so very hot that oftentimes the grains of barley leap up and are thrown out, as if the violent inflammation had made the earth throb: and in the extreme heats the inhabitants are wont to sleep upon skins filled with water. **Harpalus**, whom Alexander left there as his lieutenant and governor of that country, desiring to set forth and beautify the gardens of the king's palace and walks of the same with all manner of plants of Greece: he brought all the rest to good pass, saving ivy only, which the earth could never abide, but it ever died, because the heat and temper of the earth killed it, and the ivy of itself liketh fresh air and a cold ground. This digression is somewhat from the matter, but **peradventure** the reader will not think it troublesome, how hard soever he might find it, so it be not over-tedious.

Part Three

Alexander having won the city of Susa, he found within the castle four thousand talents *[Dryden: forty thousand]* in **ready coin**, gold and silver, besides other infinite treasure of inestimable value, amongst the which (it is said) he found to the value of five thousand talents' weight of Hermionian purple [cloth], that had been laid up there for a hundred and ninety years and yet kept its colour as fresh and lively as at first. The reason of which, they say, is that in dyeing the purple they made use of honey and of white oil in the white **tincture**, both which…preserve the clearness and brightness of their luster.

Dinon also relates that the Persian kings had water fetched from the Nile and the Danube, which they did lock up with their other treasures for a confirmation of the greatness of their empire, and to show that they were lords of the world.

Narration and Discussion

How did Alexander commemorate his victory at Gaugamela?

Why was the purple cloth considered such a treasure?

For further thought: The Persian kings seemed to have collected every kind of rich man-made treasure. But at the end of the lesson, Plutarch quotes a historian who said that Persian kings also collected natural treasures to show their ownership over the earth. If you have a nature collection, what does it mean to you? What other things might one collect that cost nothing?

Scientific narration: The naphtha demonstrations fall into the "don't try this at home" category, but older students may be interested in the technical aspects of this lesson, such as flammability.

Examination Questions for Term One

Younger Students:

1. Write an account of Alexander the Great and Bucephalus.

2. How did Alexander behave towards his physician when he was ill?

Older Students:

1. Describe (a) the meeting of Alexander with Diogenes, and (b) how Alexander crossed the Granicus River.

2. How did Alexander spend his days at a time of leisure?

3. (Alternative) Describe (a) the personal appearance, and (b) the early education of Alexander.

Lesson Thirteen

Introduction

If you are returning to the *Life of Alexander* after a break, take a few minutes to review the previous term's work, especially the victory at Gaugamela, where King Darius of Persia was defeated but escaped from the Macedonians. Remember, however, that it is more important to gain an understanding of Alexander's character than it is to recall every historical detail.

As we begin the second half of this *Life*, "the kingdom of the Persians was utterly overthrown," but the Macedonian army had not yet entered central Persia or captured Darius. **Lesson Thirteen** opens with a battle at the Persian Gates (a mountain pass leading into the central part of the country).

Vocabulary

> **by a way something about...:** by a somewhat roundabout way, but not covering too great a distance

> **sometime:** in past times

> **munificent:** generous

> **destitute:** poor

> **effaces:** erases, wipes out

People

> **Xerxes:** a great Persian king

> **Demaratus the Corinthian:** It seems likely that this is the same Demaratus who fought with Timoleon in Sicily (*Life of Timoleon*).

> **Ariobarzanes:** His name does not appear in Plutarch's text, but he was satrap (governor) of the southern part of the Persian empire, and he commanded troops at the Battle of Gaugamela. He also headed the Persian defense at the Persian Gates, but he was killed either there or

soon afterwards at Persepolis.

Thaïs: a romantic companion of Ptolemy, and possibly also of Alexander

Ptolemy I Soter: see introductory notes

Historic Occasions

330 B.C.: Battle of the Persian Gates

Reading

Part One

The entrance into Persia was through a most difficult country, and was guarded by the noblest [soldiers] of the Persians, Darius himself having escaped further. Alexander, however, chanced to find a guide in exact correspondence with what the Pythia had foretold when he was a child, that a *lycos* [wolf] should conduct him into Persia. For by such a one, whose father was a Lycian, and his mother a Persian, and who spoke both languages, he was now led into the country, **by a way something about, yet without fetching any considerable compass.**

Here a great many of the prisoners were put to the sword, of which Alexander himself gives this account, that he commanded them to be killed in the belief that it would be for his advantage. Nor was the money found here less, he says, than at Susa, besides other movables and treasure, as much as ten thousand pair of mules and five thousand camels could well carry away.

Amongst other things, he happened to observe a large statue of **Xerxes** thrown carelessly down to the ground in the confusion made by the multitude of soldiers pressing into the palace. Thereupon he stayed, and spoke unto it as if it had been alive, saying: "I cannot tell whether I should pass by thee, and let thee lie, for the war thou madest **sometime** against the Grecians; or whether I should lift thee up, respecting the noble mind and virtues thou hadst." In the end, when he had stood mute a long time, considering of it, he went his way: and, meaning to refresh his weary army, because it was the winter quarter, he remained there four months together.

The report goeth that the first time that Alexander sat under the canopy of King Darius, all of rich gold: **Demaratus the Corinthian**, who was much attached to him and had been one of his father's friends, burst out in tears for joy, good old man, saying that the Grecians long time dead before were deprived of this blessed hap, to see Alexander set in King Xerxes' princely chair.

Part Two

After that, preparing again to go against Darius, he would needs make merry one day, and refresh himself with some banquet. It chanced so, that he with his companions was bidden to a private feast, where [there were assembled his followers and some women]. Amongst them was that famous **Thaïs**, born in the country of Attica, and then mistress of **Ptolemy**, who was afterwards king of Egypt.

[As the feasting and drinking went on, Thaïs made the suggestion, half-serious, half-joking, that they should burn down Xerxes' palace to avenge his burning of the Temple of Athena in 480 B.C.]

What she said was received with such universal liking and murmurs of applause, and so seconded by the encouragement and eagerness of the company, that the king himself, persuaded to be of the party, started from his seat, and with a chaplet of flowers on his head and a torch in his hand, led them the way, while they went after him in a riotous manner, dancing and making loud cries about the place. When the rest of the Macedonians perceived it, they also in great delight ran thither with torches; for they hoped the burning and destruction of the royal palace was an argument that [Alexander] looked homeward, and had no design to reside among the barbarians. Thus some writers give their account of this action, while others say it was done deliberately; however, all agree that he soon repented of it, and commanded the fire to be quenched straight.

Part Three

Alexander was naturally most **munificent**, and grew more so as his fortune increased, accompanying what he gave with that courtesy and freedom which, to speak truth, is necessary to make a benefit really obliging.

[one example omitted for length]

[He once] met with a poor Macedonian that led a mule laden with gold of the kings: and when the poor mule was so weary that she could no longer carry her burden, the muleteer put [the burden] upon his own back, and loaded himself withal, carrying it so a good pretty way; howbeit in the end being overladen, he was about to throw it down on the ground. Alexander perceiving it, asked him what burden he carried. When it was told him: "Well," quoth he to the muleteer, "be not weary yet, but carry it into your own tent, for I give it thee." To be short, he was angrier with them that would take nothing of him, than he was with those that would ask him for something.

[omission: mature content]

The goods and riches he gave unto his familiars and guard about him were very great, as it appeareth plainly by a letter which his mother Olympias wrote unto him, to this effect: "I know thou sparest not to give thy friends large gifts, and that thou makest much of them: but thereby thou makest them king's fellows; they get many friends, and in the meantime you leave yourself **destitute**."

[further omissions]

To his mother he sent many presents but would never suffer her to meddle with matters of state or war, not indulge her busy temper, and when she fell out with him on this account, he bore her ill humour very patiently. Nay, more, when he read a long letter from Antipater full of accusations against her, "Antipater," he said, "does not know that one tear of a mother **effaces** a thousand such letters as these."

Narration and Discussion

How did Alexander's army finally get through the Persian Gates?

Was Alexander truly generous, or did he have other reasons for giving lavishly to others?

For older students: Is an action such as the slaughter of the prisoners ever justified? What does this decision show about Alexander?

Creative narration #1: As a reporter, try to get the full story about the burning of Xerxes' palace.

Creative narration #2 (for older students): If Shakespeare had written the scene where Alexander found the toppled statue of Xerxes, how might he have turned his thoughts into a monologue?

Lesson Fourteen

Introduction

This lesson continues the previous discussion of Alexander's generosity, showing examples now of the concern he showed for his friends when they were in trouble, and his scorn for those who chose pampering and luxury over courage and action. But his new status as King of Asia made things more complicated.

Vocabulary

favourites: close friends

travail: labour, work hard

vile: worthless or of little value; detestable

for slothful curiosity's sake: from squeamishness

the type: the ideal, the model

hardness: toughness, discipline

ichneumon: possibly a mythical beast known as the "enemy of the dragon"; it can also mean a mongoose or otter

hellebore: a genus of plants, often used as medicine in the ancient world, but known to be somewhat toxic

flight: escape

stayed and taken: captured

bondman: slave

Historic Occasions

324-323 B.C.: Harpalus' escape

Reading

Part One

But when Alexander perceived his **favourites** grew so luxurious and extravagant in their way of living and expenses that Hagnon the Teian wore silver nails in his shoes; that Leonnatus employed several camels only to bring him powder out of Egypt to use when he wrestled; and that Philotas had hunting nets a hundred furlongs in length; that more used precious ointment than plain oil when they went to bathe; and that they carried about servants everywhere with them to rub them and wait upon them in their chambers: he wisely and courteously rebuked them.

> "I marvel," said he, "that you, which have fought in so often and great battles, do not remember that they which **travail** do sleep more sweetly and soundly than they that take their ease and do nothing; and that you do not mark that, comparing your life with the manner of the life of the Persians, to live at pleasure is a **vile** thing, and to travail is princely. And how I pray you, can a man take pain to dress his own horse, or to make clean his lance or helmet, that **for slothful curiosity's sake** disdaineth to rub his own body with his fine fingers? Are you ignorant that **the type** of honour in all our victory consisteth in scorning to do that

which we see them do whom we have vanquished
and overcome?"

To bring them therefore by his example to acquaint themselves
with **hardness**, he took more pains in wars and in hunting, and did
hazard himself more dangerously, than ever he had done before.

[short omission]

This notwithstanding, his friends and familiars having wealth at will, as
men exceeding rich, they would needs live delicately and at ease, and
would take no more pains, misliking utterly to go up and down the
countries to make war here and there; and thereupon [they] began a
little to find fault with Alexander, and to speak evil of him. Which at
the first Alexander took quietly, saying, that it was honour for a king
to suffer himself to be slandered and ill-spoken of, for doing good.

Part Two

And yet the least good turns he did unto his friends did show his hearty
love and honour he bare them, as shall appear unto you by some
examples that follow. Peucestas, being bitten by a bear, did let his
friends understand it by letters, but he wrote nothing thereof unto
Alexander. Alexander was offended therewith and wrote unto him
thus: "Send me word at the least how thou doest, and whether any of
thy fellows did forsake thee at the hunting, to the end they may be
punished." Hephaestion being absent about certain business he had,
Alexander wrote unto him, that as they were hunting a beast called
ichneumon, Craterus unfortunately crossing Perdiccas' javelin, was
stricken through both his thighs. And upon Peucestas's recovery from
a fit of sickness, he sent a letter of thanks to his physician Alexippus.

Craterus also being sick, he dreamed of him one night, and
therefore made certain sacrifices for the recovery of his health, and
sent unto him, willing him to do the like. And when the physician
Pausanias meant to give him [Craterus] a drink of **hellebore**, he wrote
letters unto him, telling him what danger he was in, and prayed him to
be careful how he received that medicine.

He was so tender of his friends' reputations that he imprisoned
those who brought him the first news of Harpalus' **flight** and

withdrawal from his service, as if they had falsely accused him.

[omission]

It is a wonderful thing to see what pains he would take, to write for his friends, even in such trifles as he did. As when he wrote into Cilicia for a servant of Seleucus that was fled from his master, sending straight commandment that they should carefully lay for him. And by another letter he commendeth Peucestas, for that he had **stayed and taken** one Nicon, a slave of Craterus. And by one other letter also unto Megabizus, touching another **bondman** that had taken sanctuary in a temple: he commanded him also to seek to entice him out of the sanctuary, to lay hold on him if he could, but otherwise not to meddle with him in any case.

It is said also, that at the first when he used to sit in judgment to hear criminal causes, whilst the accuser went on with his complaint and accusation: he always used to lay his hand upon one of his ears while the accuser spoke, to keep it free and unprejudiced in behalf of the party accused. But afterwards, the number of accusations that were brought before him did so provoke and alter him that he did believe the false accusations, by the great number of the true that were brought in. But nothing put him more in rage than when he understood they had spoken ill of him: and then he was so fierce as no pardon would be granted, for that he loved his honour more than his kingdom or life.

Narration and Discussion

"To live at pleasure is a **vile** thing, and to **travail** is princely." Some people think quite the opposite. What did Alexander mean?

How did Alexander show that he cared for his friends? (This is a bit tricky, because one of the ways Plutarch says he showed friendship was by returning escaped slaves. Christian students might compare this with the story of Onesimus, in St. Paul's letter to Philemon.)

For older students and further thought: Charlotte Mason said that those who act with Will are those who have a purpose outside of themselves, but that those who act with Willfulness are bound by their appetites (we might say they need immediate gratification). How did Alexander's impatience with those who lived "delicately and at ease" illustrate this principle?

Creative narration: Dramatize one of the scenes from this lesson, such as Alexander's discovery of his friends' taste for luxurious living.

Lesson Fifteen

Introduction

This lesson is all about water! The Macedonians nearly perished from thirst on a long march; the last moments of King Darius' life were eased by a drink of water offered by an enemy; and Alexander reached the Caspian Sea.

Vocabulary

he went against Darius: the goal was to overtake the enemy camp

thirty-three hundred furlongs: about 412 miles (about 664 km)

in manner: practically

flying away at all adventure: running for their lives

they ran upon the spur: they rushed

almost at the last cast: almost dead

I cannot requite thee: I cannot pay you back

gave up the ghost: died

all the flower of his army: his best soldiers

People

Bessus: a Persian satrap (a high official) and military commander who conspired to capture and overthrow Darius after the Battle of Gaugamela. It appears that the conspirators intended to hand him over to Alexander; but when the Macedonians appeared at the Persian camp, they panicked, stabbed Darius, and then fled. Bessus, who was a cousin of Darius and was next in line to the throne, called himself King Artaxerxes V after the death of Darius; but he was soon captured and executed by Alexander.

Polystratus: a Macedonian soldier

Historic Occasions

330 B.C.: Death of Darius

329 B.C.: Death of Bessus

On the Map

In Part One, Alexander followed Darius into the desert area of Rhagae (east of modern-day Tehran). In Part Two, the Macedonians travelled to the region of **Hyrcania**, near the Caspian Sea (**the sea Caspium**).

Euxine: the Black Sea

Lake of Maeotis: the Sea of Azov, sometimes regarded as an extension of the Black Sea

Reading

Part One

Then at that time **he went against Darius**, thinking that he meant to fight again; but, understanding that **Bessus** had taken him, he then gave the Thessalians leave to depart home into their country, and gave them two thousand talents over and above their ordinary pay. In this long and painful pursuit of Darius, for eleven days he marched **thirty-three hundred furlongs**, (and it) harassed his soldiers so that most of them were ready to give it up, chiefly for want of water.

It chanced him one day to meet with certain Macedonians that carried (upon mules) goatskins full of water, which they had fetched from a river. They, seeing Alexander **in manner** dead for thirst, it being about noon, ran quickly to him and in a helmet brought him water. Alexander asked them to whom they carried this water. They answered him again that they carried it to their children, and said, "but yet we would have Your Grace to live: for though we lose them, we may get more children."

When they had said so, Alexander took the helmet with water, and perceiving that men of arms that were about him and had followed him did thrust out their necks to look upon this water, he gave the water back again unto them that had given it him, and thanked them, but drank none of it. "For," said he, "if I drink alone, all these men here will faint." Then they, seeing the noble courage and courtesy of Alexander, cried out that he should lead them: and therewithal began to spur their horses, saying that they were not weary nor athirst, nor did think themselves mortal, so long as they had such a king.

Every man was alike willing to follow Alexander; yet had he but [sixty] only that entered with him into the enemies' camp. There, passing over much gold and silver which was scattered abroad in the marketplace, and going also by many chariots full of women and children, which they found in the fields, **flying away at all adventure: they ran upon the spur** until they had overtaken the foremost that fled, thinking to have found Darius amongst them. But at the length, with much ado, they found him laid along in a coach, having many wounds upon his body, some of darts and some of spears. So he, being **almost at the last cast**, called for some drink, and drank cold water which **Polystratus** gave him. To whom when he had drunk, he said:

> "This is my last mishap, my friend, that having received this pleasure, **I cannot requite thee**: howbeit Alexander will recompense thee, and the gods will recompense Alexander for the liberality and courtesy which he hath shewed unto my wife and children, whom I pray thee embrace for my sake."

At these last words, he took Polystratus by the hand, and so **gave up the ghost**. Alexander came immediately after, and plainly showed that he was sorry for his death and misfortune; and undoing his own cloak, he cast it upon the body of Darius.

[omission: the cruel execution of Bessus]

Then Alexander having [laid Darius' corpse in state], he sent it unto his mother, and received his brother Exathres for one of his friends.

Part Two

And now with **the flower of his army** he marched into **Hyrcania**, where he saw a large bay of an open sea, apparently not much less than the **Euxine**, with water, however, sweeter than that of other seas, but could learn nothing of certainty concerning it, further than that in all probability it seemed to him to be an arm issuing from the **lake of Maeotis**. However, the naturalists were better informed of the truth, and had given an account of it many years before Alexander's expedition; that of four gulfs which out of the main sea enter into the continent, this, known [variously] as the Caspian and as the Hyrcanian Sea, is the most northern.

Here the barbarians, unexpectedly meeting with those who led Bucephalus, took them prisoners, and carried the horse away with them, at which Alexander was so much vexed that he sent an herald to let them know he would put them all to the sword, men, women, and children, without mercy, if they did not restore him. But on their doing so, and at the same time surrendering their cities into his hands, he not only treated them kindly, but also paid a ransom for his horse to those who took him.

Narration and Discussion

"For," said he, "if I drink alone, all these men here will faint." How did Alexander show true leadership in this situation?

Who showed the most compassion for others in this lesson?

For older students: In one sense, the conspirators had done Alexander a favour by capturing and killing Darius; and with Alexander's growing power, even Bessus might not have posed much of a threat as king of what was left of Persia, or he might have easily been conquered in battle. Discuss why it was (or was not) necessary to punish the conspirators so severely. (This could be debated in a group, or written as an editorial.)

Creative narration: Write or dramatize Alexander's reaction to the death of Darius.

Lesson Sixteen

Introduction

Scholars have debated the details of what Alexander wore as King of Asia. What did each piece of clothing symbolize to the Persians, to the Macedonians, and to Alexander himself? He did not want to be viewed as merely following Darius, so he deliberately left off the **tiara** or headdress associated with Persian kings. Median-style loose trousers made the Macedonians think of theatrical costumes, and were also sometimes worn by women, so Alexander avoided those. He did, however, incorporate a regal tunic; a Persian-style belt, which symbolized power; and a diadem crown into his wardrobe.

Vocabulary

apparel himself…: dress in the Persian style

Medes: the people of Media, a kingdom which had been conquered by the Persians. Plutarch refers here to the Median style of riding dress.

sleeved vest: loose jacket

tiara: a type of headdress associated with Persian royalty

Persian mode and the Macedonian: Plutarch's Greek text has "Median" instead of "Macedonian," and North also says "Medes," but later translators agreed that "Macedonian" made more sense.

take his own pleasure: do as he pleased

chaste and continent: well-behaved, self-controlled

People

Roxane: see introductory notes

Historic Occasions

329 B.C.: Alexander reached the Tanais/Jaxartes River

327 B.C.: Alexander married Roxane

On the Map

Parthia: a region (now part of Iran) which had belonged to the Persian Empire

river Jaxartes (Tanais): now called the Syr Darya River, in Central Asia

Reading

Part One

Departing thence, he entered into the country of **Parthia**, where, not having much to do, he began to **apparel himself after the fashion of the barbarous people,** because he thought thereby the better to win the hearts of the countrymen, framing himself unto their own fashions: or else to try the hearts of the Macedonians, to see how they would like the manner of the Persians (which he meant to bring them unto) in reverencing of him as they [the Persians] did their king, by little and little acquainting them to allow the alteration and change of his life.

This notwithstanding, he would not at the first take up the apparel of the **Medes**, which was very strange and altogether barbarous. He adopted neither the trousers nor the **sleeved vest**, nor the **tiara** for the head, but taking a middle way between the **Persian mode and the Macedonian**, so contrived his habit that it was not so flaunting as the one, and yet more pompous and magnificent than the other. At the first he did not wear it but when he would talk with the barbarous people, or else privately amongst his friends and familiars. Afterwards, notwithstanding, he showed himself openly to the people in that apparel when he gave them audience. This sight grieved the Macedonians much: but they had his virtues in such admiration, that they thought it meet in some things he should **take his own pleasure**, since he had been often hurt in the wars, and not long before had his leg broken with an arrow, and another time, had such a blow with a stone full in his neck which dimmed his sight for a good while afterwards. And yet all this could not hinder him from exposing himself freely to any dangers, insomuch that he passed the **river Jaxartes**, which he took to be the **Tanais**; and putting the Scythians to flight, followed them above a hundred furlongs, [though he was not well].

[omission for length]

Furthermore, Alexander, fearing that the Macedonians being weary with this long war, would go no further; he left all the rest of his army behind, and took only twenty thousand footmen and three thousand horsemen of the choicest men of his army, and with them invaded the country of Hyrcania. There he made an oration unto these soldiers; and told them that the barbarous people of Asia had but seen them as it were in a dream, and if they should now return back into Macedon, having but only stirred them, and not altogether subdued Asia: the people, offended with them, would set upon them as they went home *[short omission]*.

Nevertheless, he gave any man leave to return that would, merely protesting therewith against them that would go, how they did forsake him, his friends, and those who had so good hearts towards him, as to follow him in so noble a journey, to conquer the whole earth for the Macedonians. This matter is reported thus in a letter which Alexander wrote unto Antipater: and there he writeth furthermore, that having made this oration unto them, they all cried out, and bade him lead them into what part of the world he would. When they had granted their good wills, it was no hard matter afterwards, to win the rest of the common sort of soldiers who followed the example of the chiefest.

Thereupon he did frame himself the more to live after the fashion of the country there, and also to bring the men of that country unto the manner of the Macedonians: being persuaded, that by this mixture and interchange of manners one with another, he should by friendship, more than force, make them agree lovingly together, when the time came that he should be so far from the country of Persia. For this purpose, therefore, he chose thirty thousand of their children of that country, and set them to learn the Greek tongue, and to be brought up in the discipline of wars, after the Macedonian manner: and gave them schoolmasters and captains to train them in each faculty.

Part Two

And for the marrying of **Roxane**: he fancied her, seeing her at a feast where he was; which fell out as well for his turn, as if he had with better advice and counsel loved her. For the barbarous people were very proud of this match when they saw him make alliance with them in this sort, insomuch as they loved him better than they did before, because they saw in those things he was always so **chaste and continent**, that, notwithstanding, he was marvellously in love with her; yet he would not dishonourably touch this young lady before he was married unto her.

Noticing, also, that among his chief friends and favourites, Hephaestion most approved of all he did and complied with and imitated him in his change of habits; while Craterus continued strict in the observation of the customs and fashions of his own country; he made it his practice to employ the first in all transactions with the Persians, and the latter when he had to do with the Greeks or Macedonians. In general he showed more affection for Hephaestion, [but] more respect for Craterus; Hephaestion, as he used to say, being Alexander's, and Craterus the king's friend.

Hereupon these two persons bore one another a grudge in their hearts, and oftentimes broke out in open quarrel: insomuch as on a time being in India, they drew their swords and fought together, and divers of their friends ran to take part with either side. Thither came Alexander himself also, who openly before them all, bitterly took up Hephaestion, and called him fool and madman *[short omission]*.

Privately also, he sharply rebuked Craterus, and calling them both before him, he made them friends together, swearing by Jupiter Ammon, and by all the other gods, that he loved them two of all men living, nevertheless if ever he found that they fell out together again, they should both die for it, or him at the least that first began to quarrel.

So ever after that, they say, there was never foul word nor deed between them, not so much as in sport only.

[Omission for mature content]

Narration and Discussion

One reason Alexander changed his dress was "to see how [his people] would like the manner of the Persians (which he meant to bring them unto) in reverencing of him as they did their king, by little and little acquainting them to allow the alteration and change of his life." Have you ever had to begin wearing a different sort of clothes, in a new place or for a new activity? Did it make you feel like a different person? (Did other people treat you differently?)

How did Alexander stem the quarrel between his best friends?

Creative narration: Alexander's re-creation of himself as a Persian king (with modifications) might lend itself to some drama, such as a scene with his tailor.

Lesson Seventeen

Introduction

There is a lengthy omission between **Lessons Sixteen and Seventeen**, involving intrigue and misconduct in Alexander's court. It includes the execution of Philotas, the son of Parmenion; and then of Parmenion himself, an old friend who had served under King Philip. This lesson builds on the climate of fear and mistrust sparked by those events. It describes the murder of Cleitus, an act that would haunt Alexander for the rest of his life (see **Lesson Three**).

Vocabulary

Castor and Pollux: immortal brothers believed to be the patrons of travellers and sailors (giving them fair winds)

Spithridates' sword: referring to the Battle of Granicus (**Lesson Four**)

"Do you not think," said he…: Alexander's reason for saying this is not clear; but it may have been the fact that Alexander did not respond directly to his accusations which further enraged Cleitus.

Persian girdle and long white garment: belt and tunic, described in **Lesson Sixteen**

partisan: spear

prognostication: prediction

near friend of Aristotle: possibly the great-nephew of Aristotle

despising and slighting: thinking little of

censure and reproach: criticism, condemnation

audacious: bold

insinuate himself: inch or "worm" himself

austerity: stern manner

People

Cleitus (or Clitus): "Cleitus the Black" had saved Alexander's life at the Battle of the Granicus.

Callisthenes: a Greek historian, and a close friend or relative of Aristotle, who accompanied Alexander on his journey.

Anaxarchus: a philosopher

Historic Occasions

328 B.C.: Death of Cleitus

Reading

Part One

Not long after that followed the murder of Cleitus, the which to hear it simply told, would seem much more cruel than the death of Philotas. But reporting the cause and the time together in which it chanced, it will be found that it was not of set purpose, but by chance, and unfortunately, that Alexander being overcome with wine, [he] did unluckily wreak his anger upon Cleitus.

The manner of his misfortune was this: there came certain men of the low countries from the seaside, that brought apples of Greece [*Dryden: Grecian fruit*] unto Alexander. Alexander wondering to see them so green and fair, sent for Cleitus to show him them, and to give him some of them. Cleitus by chance did sacrifice at that time unto the gods, and left his sacrifice to go unto Alexander: howbeit there were three sheep that followed him, on whom the accustomed sprinklings had been done already to have sacrificed them. Alexander understanding that, told it to his soothsayers, Aristander and Cleomantis the Lacedaemonian, who both did answer him that it was [a bad omen]. Alexander thereupon gave order straight that they should do sacrifice for the health of Cleitus, and specially for that three days before he dreamed one night that he saw Cleitus in a mourning gown, sitting amongst the sons of Parmenion, the which were all dead before.

This notwithstanding, Cleitus did not make an end of his sacrifice, but came straight to supper to the king, who had that day sacrificed unto **Castor and Pollux**. And when they had drunk pretty hard, some of the company fell a-singing the verses of one Pranichus, or as others say, of Pierion, against certain captains of the Macedonians, which had not long before been overcome by the barbarous people, and only to shame them and to make the company laugh.

With these verses, ancient men that were at this feast became much offended, and grew angry with the poet that made them, and the minstrel that sang them. Alexander, on the other side, and his familiars, liked them very well, and commanded the minstrel to sing still. Cleitus, therewith, all being overtaken with wine, and besides of a churlish nature, proud and arrogant, fell into greater choler, and said that it was neither well nor honestly done in that sort to speak ill of those poor Macedonian captains (and specially amongst the barbarous people their enemies), which were far better men than they that laughed them to scorn, although their fortune was much worse than theirs. Alexander then replied, and said that, saying so, he [Cleitus] pleaded for himself, calling cowardliness "misfortune."

Then Cleitus standing up, said again:

> "But yet this my 'cowardliness' saved thy life, that
> callest thyself the son of the gods, when thou
> turnedst thy back from **Spithridates' sword**; and
> the blood which these poor Macedonians did shed
> for thee, and the wounds which they received of
> their bodies fighting for thee, have made thee so
> great, that thou disdainest now to have King Philip
> for thy father, and wilt needs make thyself the son
> of Jupiter Ammon."

Alexander being moved with these words, straight replied: "O villain, thinkest thou to escape unpunished for these proud words of thine, which thou usest continually against me, making the Macedonians rebel against Alexander?"

Cleitus answered again, "Too much are we punished, Alexander, for our pains and service to receive such reward: nay, most happy think we them that long since are dead and gone, not now to see the Macedonians scourged with rods of the Medes and compelled to curry favour with the Persians to have access unto the king."

Thus, Cleitus boldly speaking against Alexander, and Alexander again answering and reviling him: the gravest men sought to pacify this stir and tumult. Alexander then turning himself unto Xenodochus the Cardian and Artemius the Colophonian: **"Do you not think," said he, "that the Grecians are, amongst the Macedonians, as demi-gods that walk among brute beasts?"**

Cleitus for all this would not give over, but cried out, and bade Alexander speak openly what he had to say, or else not to bid free men come to sup with him that were wont to speak frankly: if not, to keep with the barbarous slaves that honoured his **Persian girdle and his white tunic**.

Which words so provoked Alexander that, not able to suppress his anger any longer, he threw one of the apples that lay upon the table at him, and hit him, and then looked about for his sword. But Aristophanes, one of his life-guard, had hid that out of the way. And when every man came straight about him to stay him, and to pray him to be contented: he immediately rose from the board and called his guard unto him in the Macedonian tongue (which was a sign of great trouble to follow after it) and commanded a trumpeter to sound the alarm. But he, drawing back, would not sound: whereupon Alexander struck him with his fist. Notwithstanding, the trumpeter was greatly commended afterwards for disobeying an order which would have put the whole army into tumult and confusion.

All this could not quiet Cleitus, whereupon his friends with much ado thrust him out of the hall: but he came in again at another door, very irreverently and confidently singing the verses out of Euripides's *Andromache*:

> In Greece, alas! How ill things ordered are!

Then Alexander taking a **partisan** from one of his guard, as Cleitus was coming towards him, and had lifted up the hanging before the door, he ran him through the body, so that Cleitus fell to the ground, and fetching one groan, died presently.

Part Two

Alexander's choler had left him straight, and he became marvellous sorrowful: and when he saw his friends round about him say never a word, he plucked the partisan out of his [Cleitus'] body, and would have thrust it into his own throat. Howbeit his guard about him caught him by the hands and carried him perforce into his chamber: and there he did nothing all that night but weep bitterly, and the next day following, until such time as he was able to cry no more, but lying on the ground, only lay sighing.

His friends hearing his voice no more, were afraid, and came into his chamber by force to comfort him. But Alexander would hear none of them, saving Aristander the soothsayer, who remembered him of his dream he had of Cleitus before, which was a **prognostication** of that which had happened: whereby it appeared that it was his destiny before he was born. This seemed to comfort Alexander.

They now brought **Callisthenes** the philosopher (the **near friend** of Aristotle) and **Anaxarchus** of Abdera to him. Callisthenes used moral language, and gentle and soothing means, hoping to find access for words of reason, and get ahold upon the passion. But Anaxarchus, who had always taken a course of his own in philosophy, and had a name for **despising and slighting** his contemporaries, as soon as he came in cried out aloud,

> "Is this the Alexander whom the whole world looks
> to, lying here weeping like a slave for fear of the
> **censure and reproach** of men, to whom he
> himself ought to be a law and measure of equity, if
> he would use the right his conquests have given him
> as supreme lord and governor of all, and not be the
> victim of a vain and idle opinion? Do you not
> know," said he, "that Jupiter is represented to have
> Justice and Law on each hand of him, to signify that
> all the actions of a conqueror are lawful and just?"

With these and the like speeches, Anaxarchus indeed allayed the king's grief, but withal corrupted his character, rendering him more **audacious** and lawless than he had been. Nor did he fail by these means to **insinuate** himself into his favour, and to make Callisthenes' company, which at all times because of his **austerity** was not very acceptable, more uneasy and disagreeable to him.

Narration and Discussion

Had Alexander lost his principles (such as devotion to his friends), or was this simply an unfortunate event caused by too much drink?

How did the words of Anaxarchus soothe away the king's guilt, but also "corrupt his character?" Can you think of real-life or literary examples where facing an uncomfortable truth has led to repentance? (A Bible verse to look up: Proverbs 28:23.)

Creative narration: Dramatize (or write the script for) the scene between Alexander and the philosophers.

Lesson Eighteen

Introduction

The last lesson told the story of Cleitus, Alexander's old friend who was killed as a result both of his own temper and the king's increasingly unstable nature. Now we read about another man who paid a similar price, but this time for his unwillingness to compromise his deepest principles.

Vocabulary

at King Alexander's board: at his dinner table

touching the seasons…: talking about the weather

galled Anaxarchus to the quick: stung him to the heart

estimation: good status, reputation

an oration *extempore*: an unrehearsed speech

inveighing: protesting, complaining

odious to them: hated by them

Hermolaus' conspiracy: Alexander's page Hermolaus conspired with others to assassinate the king, in revenge for a certain punishment. Hermolaus blamed **Callisthenes** for suggesting the idea.

engaged in the design: involved in the conspiracy

brought up with him: brought up in Aristotle's house

kinsman: relative

apprehended: arrested, seized

Historic Occasions

327 B.C.: the conspiracy of Hermolaus, while the army was in Bactria

On the Map

Bactria: a region of Central Asia, corresponding to present-day
Afghanistan

Reading

Part One

It is written also that there was certain talk one night **at King
Alexander's board touching the seasons of the year, and
temperateness of the air**, and that Callisthenes was of the opinion
which maintained that the country they were in at that time was much
colder, and the winter also sharper, than in Greece. Anaxarchus held
the contrary opinion, and stiffly maintained it, insomuch as
Callisthenes said unto him: "And yet must thou grant, that it is colder
here than there. For there you used to have but one threadbare cloak
to keep out the coldest winter, and here you have three good warm
mantles one over another."

This **galled Anaxarchus to the quick** and made him more angry
than before; and for the other rhetoricians and flatterers, they did also
hate him [Callisthenes], because they saw him followed by young men
for his eloquence, and beloved also of old men for his honest life, the
which was very grave, modest, and contented with his own, desiring
no man's else. Whereby men found that the reason he alleged for
following of Alexander in this voyage was true: for he said that he came
to be a humble suitor to the king, to restore his banished citizens into
their country again, and to replenish their city with inhabitants.

Now, though [Callisthenes'] **estimation** made him chiefly to be
envied; yet did he himself give his enemies occasion to accuse him. For
oftentimes being invited by the king to supper, either he would not
come, or if he came, he would be mute, and say nothing, showing by
his gravity and silence that nothing pleased him that was either said or
done. Whereupon Alexander himself said on a time unto him:

I cannot think that person wise,

That in his own case hath no eyes.

Being with many more invited to sup with the king, he was called upon when the cup came to him, to make **an oration *extempore*** in praise of the Macedonians; and he did it with such a flow of eloquence, that all who heard it rose from their seats to clap and applaud him, and threw their garland upon him; only Alexander told him out of Euripides:

> It is no mastery to be eloquent,

> In handling of a plenteous argument.

"Therefore," said he, "if you will show the force of your eloquence, tell my Macedonians their faults, and dispraise them, that by hearing their errors they may learn to be better for the future." Callisthenes presently obeyed him, retracting all he had said before, and, **inveighing** against the Macedonians with great freedom, added that Philip thrived and grew powerful chiefly by the discord of the Grecians, alleging these verses:

> Where discord reigns in realm or town,

> Even wicked folk do win renown;

which so offended the Macedonians, that he was **odious** to them ever after.

[omission for length]

Part Two

Therefore when **Hermolaus' conspiracy** came to be discovered, the charges which [Callisthenes'] enemies brought against him were the more easily believed, particularly that when the young man asked him what he should do to be the most illustrious person on earth, he told him the readiest way was to kill him who was already so; and that to incite him to commit the deed, he bade him not be awed by the golden couch, but remember Alexander was a man equally infirm and vulnerable as another. However, none of Hermolaus' accomplices, in the utmost extremity, made any mention of Callisthenes' being **engaged in the design**. And Alexander himself also writing of this treason immediately after, unto Craterus, Attalus, and Alcetas, said that their servants which had been racked and put to the torture did constantly affirm that they only had conspired his death, and no man else was privy unto it.

But afterwards, he sent another letter unto Antipater, wherein he directly accused Callisthenes, and said that his servants [*Dryden: the young men*] had already been stoned to death by the Macedonians; howbeit that he himself would afterwards also punish the master, and those that had sent unto him and that had received the murderers into their cities, who came of purpose to kill him. And therein he plainly showed the ill-will he bore unto Aristotle, for that Callisthenes had been **brought up with him**, being his **kinsman**.

Callisthenes' death is variously related. Some say he was hanged by Alexander's orders; others, that he died of sickness in prison; but Chares writes he was kept in chains seven months after he was **apprehended**, on purpose that he might be proceeded against in full council, when Aristotle should be present; and that growing very fat, and contracting a disease of vermin, he there died about the time that Alexander was wounded in India.

[omission for length]

Narration and Discussion

Callisthenes was "followed by young men for his eloquence, and beloved also of old men for his honest life." How did he end up in such deep trouble and with such a sad death?

Alexander told Callisthenes that it took no great skill to make a speech praising his men; but that it would be a much greater feat to "dispraise" them. Why do you think Callisthenes agreed to this challenge? Would you have done so?

Lesson Nineteen

Introduction

Alexander's journey to India grew out of his desire to conquer the entire known world. From a historical standpoint, we run into some limitations and difficulties with Plutarch's version of the story. One problem is that other authors, such as Arrian in his *Anabasis*, covered the Indian campaign in more detail than Plutarch did. Another is that later historians have re-examined the earlier accounts, trying to determine what details were most likely true, and which ones may have been exaggerated or simply misunderstood. One example is Alexander's granting of kingdoms to Porus in **Lesson Twenty**; in fact, Porus probably ruled that territory already.

For the purposes of this study, we will confine ourselves to the story as the "moral biographer" Plutarch tells it. But those who wish to go deeper will find no shortage of material!

Vocabulary

laden with spoils: weighed down with treasure

victuals: food

the fortress of Sisimithres: also called the Sogdian Rock

in recompense thereof: as payment or reward

capitulation: surrender, ceasing to resist

the choice of his horsemen: his best cavalry officers

twenty furlongs: 2.5 miles (about 4 km)

four cubits and a span high: about seven feet (2 m) tall

People

Oxyartes: a nobleman of Bactria, and the father of **Roxane**

Taxiles: the ruler of a region in the Punjab, of which the capital city was **Taxila**. His proper name was Ambhi, but the Greek chroniclers called him Taxiles/Taxilas. He took part in the **Battle of the Hydaspes**, and was involved first in pursuit of and then in negotiations with **Porus**.

Porus [Poros]: the ruler of a neighbouring region, who was not on good terms with Taxiles.

Historic Occasions

326 B.C.: Battle of the **Hydaspes River**, against Porus

On the Map

Referring to a map of Alexander's journeys in **India** will be helpful. (A useful search term is "Indian campaign of Alexander the Great.")

city of Nysa: Nisatta, located in present-day Pakistan

River of Hydaspes: the Jhelum River

Reading

Part One

Alexander, now intent upon his expedition into **India**, took notice that his soldiers were so **laden with spoils** that it hindered their marching. Therefore, at break of day, as soon as the baggage wagons were laden, first he set fire to his own, and to those of his friends, and then commanded those to be burnt which belonged to the rest of the army: an act which in the deliberation of it had seemed more dangerous and difficult than it proved in the execution, with which few were dissatisfied; for most of the soldiers, as if they had been inspired, uttering loud outcries and warlike shoutings, supplied one another with what was absolutely necessary, and burnt and destroyed all that was superfluous, the sight of which redoubled Alexander's zeal and eagerness for his design.

And, indeed, this made Alexander much more severe than he was before, besides that he was already become cruel enough; and without mercy or pardon he did sharply punish every man that offended. For having commanded Menander, one of his friends, to keep him a fortress, he put him to death, because he would not remain there. Furthermore, he himself slew Orsodates (a captain of the barbarous people) with a javelin, for that he rebelled against him.

[omission: certain signs and omens]

93

And truly so did he sustain many dangers in those wars and was oftentimes hurt in fight. But the greatest loss he had of his men was for lack of **victuals**, and by the infection of the air. For he, striving to overcome Fortune by valiantness, and her force by virtue, thought nothing impossible for a valiant man, neither anything able to withstand a noble heart.

It is reported, that when he went to besiege **[the fortress of Sisimithres]**, it being thought unassaultable, and that his soldiers were in despair of it, he asked **Oxyartes** what heart Sisimethres had. Oxyartes answered him, that he was the veriest coward in the world. "O, that is well," quoth Alexander: "then it is to be won, if that be true thou sayest, since the captain of the fortress is but a coward." So he took it of a sudden, by putting Sisimethres in a great fear.

After that also, he did besiege another fortress of as great strength and difficulty to assault as the other, and making the young soldiers of the Macedonians to go to the assault, he called one of them unto him, whose name also was Alexander, unto whom he said thus: "Alexander, this day thou must fight like a man, and it be but for thy namesake." The young man did not forget his words, for he fought so valiantly, that he was slain, for whom Alexander was very sorry.

Another time when his men were afraid, and dared not come near unto the **city of Nysa** to assault it, because there ran a very deep river hard by the walls: he came to the riverside, and said: "Oh, what a coward am I, that never learned to swim!" and so prepared himself to swim over upon his shield. Here, after the assault was over, the ambassadors who, from several towns which he had blocked up, came to submit to him and make their peace, were surprised to find him still in his armour, without anyone in waiting or attendance upon him; and when at last someone brought him a cushion, he made the eldest of them, named Acuphis, take it and sit down upon it.

Acuphis marvelling at Alexander's great courtesy, asked him what they should do for him, thenceforth to be his good friends. "I will," said Alexander, "that they from whom thou comest as ambassador unto us do make thee their king: and withal that they do send me a hundred of their best men for hostages." Acuphis, smiling, answered him again: "But I shall rule them better, king, if I send you the worst, and not the best."

Part Two

The extent of **King Taxiles'** dominions in India was thought to be as large as Egypt, abounding in good pastures, and producing beautiful fruits. The king himself had the reputation of a wise man, and at his first interview with Alexander he spoke to him in these terms:

> "What should we need, Alexander, to fight, and
> make wars one with another, if thou comest not to
> take away our water, and our necessary commodity
> to live by: for which things, men of judgment must
> needs fight? As for other goods, if I be richer than
> thou, I am ready to give thee of mine: and if I have
> less, I will not think scorn to thank thee, if thou wilt
> give me some of thine."

This discourse pleased Alexander so much that, embracing him, [he said]:

> "Thinkest thou this meeting of ours can be without
> fight, for all these goodly fair words? No, no, thou
> hast won nothing by that: for I will fight and
> contend with thee in honesty and courtesy, because
> thou shalt not exceed me in bounty and liberality."

So Alexander taking divers gifts of him, but giving more unto Taxiles: he drank to him one night at supper, and said, "I drink to thee a thousand talents in gold." This gift misliked Alexander's friends: but **in recompense thereof**, he won the hearts of many of those barbarous lords and princes of that country.

But the best soldiers of the Indians now entering into the pay of several of the cities, undertook to defend them, and did it so bravely, that they put Alexander to a great deal of trouble, till at last, after a **capitulation**, upon the surrender of the place, he fell upon them as they were marching away, and put them all to the sword. This one breach of his word remains as a blemish upon his achievements in war, which he otherwise had performed throughout with that justice and honour that became a king. Nor was he less incommoded by the Indian philosophers, who inveighed against those princes who joined his party, and solicited the free nations to oppose him. He took several of these also and caused them to be hanged.

Part Three

Alexander, in his own letters, has given us an account of his war with Porus. He says that, both their camps lying on either side of the **River of Hydaspes**, King Porus set his elephants upon the bank of the river with their heads towards their enemies, to keep them from passing over: and that he himself did continually make a noise and tumult in his camp, to acquaint his men not to be afraid of the barbarous people.

Furthermore, that in a dark night when there was no moonlight, he took part of his footmen, and **the choice of his horsemen**, and went far from his enemies to get over into a little island. When he was come into the island, there fell a wonderful shower of rain, great winds, lightnings and thunders upon his camp, insomuch as he saw many of his men burnt by lightning in this little island. He nevertheless quitted the island and made over to the other side.

The river being swollen with the great flood of rain that fell the night before, overflowing the banks, it did eat into the ground where the water ran: so that Alexander when he had passed over the river, and was come to the other side, found himself in very ill case, for that he could hardly keep his feet, because the earth was very slippery under him, and the rage of the water had eaten into it, and broken it down on every side. It is written of him, that then he said unto the Athenians, "O ye Athenians, will ye believe what dangers I incur to merit your praise?" Thus Onesicritus reporteth it.

Alexander says (that) here the men left their boats, and passed the breach in their armour, up to the breast in water, and that then he advanced with his horse about **twenty furlongs** before his foot soldiers, concluding that if the enemy charged him with their cavalry, he should be too strong for them; and if with their foot soldiers, his own would come up in time enough to his assistance. Nor did he judge amiss; for being charged by a thousand horse and sixty armed chariots, which advanced before their main body, he took all the chariots, and killed four hundred horse upon the place. King Porus then knowing by those signs that Alexander was there in person, and that he had passed over the river: he marched towards him with all his army in battle array, saving a few which he left behind to hold the rest of the Macedonians in play, if they should attempt to pass the river.

Alexander, being afraid of the great multitude of his enemies, and of the terror of the elephants, did not give charge upon the midst of the battle; but being himself in the left wing, he gave charge upon the corner of the enemy's left wing, and also commanded them that were in the right wing to do the like. So, both the ends of the enemy's army were broken and put to flight; and they that fled ran unto the elephants and gathered themselves together about them.

Thus, the battle being begun, the conflict continued long, insomuch as the enemies were scantly all overthrown by three of the clock in the afternoon. Almost all the historians agree in relating that Porus was **four cubits and a span high,** and that when he was upon his elephant, which was of the largest size, his stature and bulk were so answerable, that he appeared to be proportionably mounted as a horseman on his horse. This elephant did show great wit and care, to save the king his master. For whilst he perceived his master was strong enough, he lustily repulsed those which came to assail him: but when he found that he began to faint, having many wounds upon his body, and arrows sticking in it: then being afraid lest his master should fall down from his back, he softly fell on his knees, and gently taking his darts and arrows with his trunk, which he had in his body, he plucked them all from him one after another.

Narration and Discussion

Alexander was said to be more severe (North says "rigorous") than he had been before. Give some evidence of this. Why do you think he had become harsher and less forgiving?

Tell about the battle Alexander fought with Porus.

For older students: Alexander said that there was nothing "able to withstand a noble heart." Do you agree?

Lesson Twenty

Introduction

After the victorious but costly battle at Hydaspes, Alexander wanted to continue the campaign, and to cross the Ganges River. However, his men refused to go on, either from homesickness and exhaustion, or from embarrassment that they had had so much difficulty fighting a minor ruler like Porus. Alexander was forced to agree to head back.

Vocabulary

satrap: governor

bits of bridles: part of the horses' reins

veneration: awe, reverence

rampart: defensive wall

scimitar: curved sword

mortally: fatally, to death

he was taken…: he was unconscious and seemed almost dead

On the Map

Alexander's troops continued to the southwest, following the **Indus River** to the **Arabian Sea**.

city of the Mallians: The Mallians are thought to be the Malavas (or Malwas), a tribe which had settled in the Punjab region

Reading

Part One

Porus being taken, Alexander asked him how he should handle him. "Princely," answered Porus. *[Dryden: "As a king."]* Alexander asked him again, if he would say anything else. "I comprehend all," said he, "in this word 'princely.'" And Alexander, accordingly, not only suffered him to govern his own kingdom as **satrap** under himself, but he gave him also the additional territory of various independent tribes whom he subdued, a district which, it is said, contained fifteen several nations and five thousand considerable towns, besides abundance of villages. To another government, three times as large as this, he appointed Philip, one of his friends.

His horse Bucephalus died at this battle, not in the field, but afterwards whilst he was in cure for the wounds he had on his body; but as Onesicritus saith, he died even worn for very age. Alexander was as sorry for his death as if he had lost any of his familiar friends; and for proof thereof, he built a great city in the place where his horse was buried, upon the river of Hydaspes, the which he called after his name, Bucephalusia *[short omission]*.

This last battle against King Porus killed the Macedonians' hearts, and made them that they had no desire to go any further to conquer India.

[omission for length]

Alexander, offended with his men's refusal, kept close in his tent for certain days, and lay upon the ground, saying that he did not thank them for all that they had done already, unless they passed over the River of Ganges also: and that to return back again, it was as much as to confess that he had been overcome. At the length, when he saw and considered that there was great reason in his friends' persuasions which laboured to comfort him, and that his soldiers came to the door of his tent, crying and lamenting, humbly beseeching him to lead them back again: in the end he took pity of them, and was contented to return.

This notwithstanding, before he departed from those parts, he put forth many vain and false devices to make his name immortal among that people. He made armours of greater proportion than his own, and mangers for horses, higher than the common sort: moreover, he made **bits of bridles** also far heavier than the common sort and made them to be thrown and scattered abroad in every place. He built great altars also in honour of the gods, the which the kings of the Praesians have in great **veneration** at this day: and passing over the river, do make sacrifices there, after the manner of the Grecians.

[omission for length]

Part Two

Alexander was now eager to see the ocean. To which purpose he caused a great many rowboats and rafts to be built, in the which he easily went down the rivers at his pleasure. Howbeit, this his pleasant going by water was not without war: for he would land oftentimes, and did assail cities, and conquered all as he went. Yet in assailing the **city of the Mallians** (which they say are the warlikest men of all the Indians), he was almost slain there.

For, having repulsed the enemies from the wall, he himself was the first man that set foot on a ladder to get up, the which brake as soon as ever he was gotten upon the **rampart**. Then the barbarous people coming together against the wall, did throw darts at him from beneath, and many times lighted upon him. Alexander, having few of his men about him, made no more ado but leaped down from the wall in the midst of his enemies, and by good hap lighted on his feet. His harness making a great noise with the fall, the barbarous people were afraid, thinking they had seen some light or spirit go before him: so that at the first they all betook them to their legs, and ran scatteringly here and there.

Till seeing him seconded but by two of his guards, they fell upon him hand to hand, and some, while he bravely defended himself, tried to wound him through his armour with their swords and spears. And one who stood further off drew a bow with such just strength that the arrow, finding its way through his [armour], stuck in his ribs under the breast. This stroke was so violent that it made him give back, and set one knee to the ground upon which the man ran up with his drawn **scimitar**, thinking to dispatch him, and [would] have done it, if Peucestas and Limnaeus had not interposed, who were both wounded, Limnaeus **mortally**, but Peucestas stood his ground, while Alexander killed the barbarians.

But this did not free him from danger; for, besides many other wounds, at last he received so weighty a stroke of a club upon his neck that he was forced to lean his body against the wall, still, however, facing the enemy. At this extremity, the Macedonians made their way in and gathered round him. They took him up, just as he was fainting away, having lost all sense of what was done near him, and conveyed him to his tent, upon which it was present reported all over the camp that he was dead. But when they had with great difficulty and pains sawed off the shaft of the arrow, which was of wood, and so with much trouble got off his armour, they came to cut the head of it, which was three fingers broad and four long, and stuck fast in the bone. During the operation **he was taken with almost mortal swoonings**, but when it was out he came to himself again.

Yet though all danger was past, he continued very weak, and confined himself a great while to a regular diet and the method of his cure: until he heard the Macedonians cry, and make great noise about his tent, desirous to see him. Then he took his cloak and came out amongst them all: and after he had done sacrifice unto the gods for recovery of his health, he went on his journey again, and in the same did conquer many great countries and took divers goodly cities.

Narration and Discussion

"...he put forth many vain and false devices to make his name immortal among that people." How did Alexander himself contribute to romantic legends about his greatness?

What may have been some of the reasons that Alexander was less successful in India than he had been elsewhere?

Lesson Twenty-One

Introduction

Part One of this lesson is a dialogue about philosophical conundrums. Those working in groups might enjoy acting it out.

Part Two describes the continuing travels of Alexander's army.

Vocabulary

pertinent: this can be translated "correct"

going still through the country: as explained in the next sentence, they created a "travelling banquet"

rising up of height: the meaning of this is not clear

flutes and shawms: musical instruments

fooling: dancing, drinking, and revelry

Historic Occasions

324 B.C.: Alexander returned to Persia

On the Map

Beginning the journey back to Macedonia, the army moved westward, following the Arabian Sea coast. They then travelled northwest through the countries of **Gedrosia** and **Carmania**.

Sea Oceanum: This is a translation of the Latin "Mare Oceanum" or "World-Encircling Ocean." It referred to exactly that: the Atlantic Ocean, which surrounded the known world.

island called Scillustis: an island near the mouth of the Indus River, which likely no longer exists

Reading

Part One

In this voyage, (Alexander) took ten Indian philosophers prisoner, who had been most active in persuading Sabbas to revolt [in 325 B.C.], and who had caused the Macedonians a great deal of trouble. These men, called Gymnosophists, were reputed to be extremely ready and succinct in their answers, which he made trial of by putting difficult questions to them, letting them know that those whose answers were not **pertinent** should be put to death; of which he made the eldest of them judge.

The question he asked the first man was this:

1. Whether the dead or the living were the greater number. He answered, the living. "For the dead," said he, "are no more men."

2. The second man he asked: whether the earth, or the sea brought forth most creatures. He answered, the earth. "For the sea," said he, "is but a part of the earth."

3. To the third man: which of all beasts was the subtlest. "That," said he, "which man hitherto never knew."

4. To the fourth: why did he make Sabbas rebel? "Because," said he, "he should live honourably, or die vilely."

5. To the fifth, which he thought was first, the day, or the night? He answered, "the day, by a day." The king, finding his answer strange, added to this speech: "Strange questions must needs have strange answers."

6. Coming to the sixth man, he asked him how a man should come to be beloved. "If he be a good man," said he, "not terrible."

7. To the seventh, how a man should be a god? "In doing a thing," said he, "impossible for a man."

8. To the eight, which was the stronger: life or death? "Life," said he, "that suffereth so many troubles."

9. And unto the ninth and last man: how long a man should live? "Until," said he, "he think it better to die, than to live."

When Alexander had heard these answers, he turned unto the judge, and bade him give his judgment upon them. The judge said that they had all answered one worse than another.

"Then shalt thou die first," said Alexander, "because thou hast given such sentence."

"Not so, O King," replied the gymnosophist, "unless you said falsely that he should die first who made the worst answer."

In conclusion Alexander gave them presents and dismissed them.

[omission for length]

Part Two

Alexander continued seven months travelling upon the rivers, to go see the great **Sea Oceanum**. Then he took ship, and sailed into a little **island called Scillustis**, howbeit others call it Psiltucis. There he landed, made sacrifices unto the gods, and viewed the greatness and nature of the sea Oceanum, and all the situation of the coast upon that sea, as far as he could go.

[omission for length: some difficult travels]

After sixty days' march he came into **Gedrosia**, where he found great plenty of all things, which the neighbouring kings and governors of provinces, hearing of his approach, had taken care to provide. After he had refreshed his army there a little, he went through the country of **Carmania**, where he continued seven days together banqueting, **going still through the country**. For night and day, he was feasting continually with his friends upon a platform erected on a scaffold longer than broad, **rising up of height**, and drawn with eight goodly horses. After that scaffold followed divers other chariots covered over, some covered with purple and embroidered canopies, and some with green boughs, which were continually supplied afresh: and in those were Alexander's other friends and captains with garlands of flowers upon their heads, which drank and made merry together. Here was now no helmet, pike, dart, nor target seen: but gold and silver bowls, cups, and flagons in the soldiers' hands, all the way as they went, drawing wine out of great pipes and vessels which they carried with them, one drinking to another, some marching in the fields going forward, and others also set at the table. About them were the minstrels playing and piping on their **flutes and shawms**, and women singing and dancing, and **fooling** by the way as they went.

[omission: mature content]

Narration and Discussion

In Part One, which was your favourite answer of the nine? (**Creative narration:** find a way to expand on it, through art, poetry, or drama.)

How did the tenth philosopher show that he was the wisest of all?

Lesson Twenty-Two

Introduction

Alexander, in spite of the travelling party described in the previous lesson, had suffered setbacks during his time in India. Many men had died, and the army was in such a weak state that cities he had "conquered" were rebelling. People in Macedonia thought (happily or sadly) that he would never return from his journey. But Alexander was not ready to give up the territory he had claimed, or his dream of a triumphant return. He even took the opportunity to get married.

Vocabulary

he resolved himself to sail…: this voyage was planned, but did not take place

great insolencies…: the governors were growing rich by overtaxing their people

broil and sedition: turmoil, uprisings

a faction against Antipater: Antipater had been left to govern during Alexander's absence

a crown: a piece of gold

People

Cyrus: Cyrus the Great, who lived in the sixth century B.C., was the founder of the Persian empire.

Antigonus: a Macedonian general; see introductory notes

Historic Occasions

324 B.C.: Alexander returned to Persia and married Statira

On the Map

Thapsacus: a town on the Euphrates (in modern-day Syria)

Reading

Part One

At Gedrosia, Aleander's admiral, Nearchus, came to him and delighted him so with the narrative of his voyage, that **he resolved himself to sail** out of the mouth of the Euphrates with a great fleet, with which he designed to go round by Arabia and Africa, and so by Hercules' Pillars into the Mediterranean; in order for which he directed all sorts of vessels to be built at **Thapsacus,** and made provision everywhere of seamen and pilots.

But now the difficulty of the journey which he took upon him for the conquest of India, the danger he was in when he fought with the Mallians, and the number of his men which he lost besides which was very great; all these things considered together made men believe that he should never return with safety. They made all the people (which he had conquered) bold to rise against him and gave his governors and lieutenants of provinces occasion to commit **great insolencies, robberies, and exactions** of people. To be short, it put all his kingdom in **broil and sedition.** Even at home, Olympias and Cleopatra had raised **a faction against Antipater,** and divided his government between them, Olympias seizing upon Epirus, and Cleopatra upon Macedonia. When Alexander was told of it, he said his mother had made the best choice, for the Macedonians would never endure to be ruled by a woman.

Thereupon he sent Nearchus back again to the sea, determining to fill all the seacoasts with war. As he travelled through the countries far from the sea, he put his captains and governors to death which had revolted against him *[short omission]*.

Part Two

As he came through the country of Persia, he first renewed the old custom there, which was that when the kings did return home from any far journey, they gave unto every woman **a crown** apiece. It is said therefore that for this cause, some of their natural kings many times did not return again into their country *[short omission]*.

Then finding **Cyrus's** sepulcher opened and rifled, he put Polymachus, who did it, to death, though he was a man of some distinction, a born Macedonian of Pella. When he had read the inscription written upon it in the Persian tongue, he would needs also have it written in the Greek tongue: and this it was:

> "O man, what so thou art, and whencesoever thou comest, for I know thou shalt come: I am Cyrus that conquered the Empire of Persia, and I pray thee envy me not for this little earth that covereth my body."

These words pierced Alexander's heart, when he considered the uncertainty of worldly things.

[omitted: the suicide of Calanus the philosopher]

At Susa, he married Darius's daughter Statira, and celebrated also the nuptials of his friends, bestowing the noblest of the Persian ladies upon the worthiest of them, at the same time making it an entertainment in honour of the other Macedonians whose marriages had already taken place. At this feast, it is written that, nine thousand persons sitting at the boards, he gave unto every one of them a cup of gold to offer wine in honour of the gods. And there also, amongst other wonderful gifts, he did pay all the debts the Macedonians owed unto their creditors, the which amounted unto the sum of ten thousand talents saving a hundred and thirty less.

Whereupon **Antigonus**, who had lost one of his eyes, though he owed nothing, got his name set down in the list of those who were in debt, and bringing one who pretended to be his creditor, and to have supplied him from the bank, received the money. But when the cheat was found out, the king was so incensed at it, that he banished him from court, and took away his command, though he was an excellent soldier and a man of great courage. For when he was but a young man, he was shot into the eye, before the city of Perinthus, which King Philip did besiege: and at that present time they would have plucked the arrow out of his eye, but he never fainted for it, neither would suffer them to pull it out, before he had first driven his enemies within the walls of their city. Accordingly, he was not able to support such a disgrace with any patience, and it was plain that grief and despair would have made him kill himself, but that the king fearing it, not only pardoned him, but bade him besides keep the money which was given him.

Narration and Discussion

How did Alexander show that he still valued generosity?

Antigonus appears to have been a bit of a scoundrel. Why did Alexander let him off the hook?

For older students: Compare Alexander's reaction to the inscription about Cyrus to the previous discussion with the Gymnosophists. What may have been going through his mind?

Lesson Twenty-Three

Introduction

Alexander remained at Susa for a time, although Plutarch also mentions a trip to **Ecbatana**. He then prepared to travel westward to Babylon, not knowing it would be his last journey.

Vocabulary

thirty thousand boys: see **Lesson Sixteen**, Part Two

sick and impotent: those who were physically unable to serve

they let fall their stoutness: they let go of their stubbornness

naked in their shirts: this showed their humility

capon: a male chicken that has been neutered

tennis: this is North's translation; some sort of ball game

diadem: royal crown (sometimes in the form of a headband)

irons: chains

Aristotle's quiddities to argue pro and contra: Alexander, having studied with Aristotle, recognized his methods of argument

People

Antipater, Iolaus, Cassander.: see introductory notes

Historic Occasions

October, 324 B.C.: Death of Hephaestion

On the Map

Media (Medes): a region of northwestern Iran

Babylon: an ancient city of southern Mesopotamia

Reading

Part One

The **thirty thousand boys**, whom he left behind him to be taught and disciplined, were so improved at his return (to Persia), both in strength and beauty, and (they) performed their exercises with such dexterity and wonderful agility, that Alexander rejoiced when he saw them. This, notwithstanding, did much discourage the Macedonians, and made them greatly afraid, because they thought that from henceforth the king would make less account of them.

For when Alexander would have sent the **sick and impotent** persons, which had been maimed in the wars, into the low country, to the seaside: they answered him, that so doing he should do them great wrong, to send these poor men from him in that sort (after they had done him all the service they could) home to their country and friends, in worse case than he took them from thence. And therefore, they said, if he would send away some, let him send them all away as men unserviceable, specially since he had now such goodly young dancers about him with whom he might go conquer the world.

Alexander was marvellously offended with their proud words, insomuch that in his anger he reviled them all, put away his ordinary guard, and took Persians in their place, making some the guard about his own person, and others his ushers, heralds, and ministers to execute his will and commandment.

The poor Macedonians, seeing Alexander thus waited on, and themselves so shamefully rejected, **they let fall their stoutness**, and after they had communed of the matter together, they were ready to tear themselves for spite and malice. In fine when they had laid their heads together, they consented to go unto his tent and without weapons, **naked in their shirts** to yield themselves unto him, weeping and howling, beseeching him to do with them what pleased him, and to use them like wretched unthankful creatures.

But Alexander, though his anger was now somewhat pacified, did not receive them the first time; neither did they also go their ways, but remained there two days and nights together, in this pitiful state, before the door of his tent, lamenting unto him, and calling him their sovereign and king: until that he came himself out of his tent the third day, and seeing the poor wretches in this grievous and pitiful state, he himself fell a-weeping a long time. So, after he had a little rebuked them, he called them courteously, and gave the impotent and sick persons leave to depart home, rewarding them very honourably. Furthermore, he wrote unto **Antipater** his lieutenant that he should always give them the highest place in all common sports and assemblies, and that they should be crowned with garlands of flowers. Moreover, he commanded that the orphans whose parents were slain in the wars should receive the pay of their fathers.

Part Two

After Alexander was come unto the city of Ecbatana, in the kingdom of **Media**, and that he had dispatched his weightiest causes: he gave himself again unto public sports, feasts, and pastimes, for that there were newly come unto him, out of Greece, three thousand excellent masters and devisers of such sports. But they were soon interrupted by Hephaestion's falling sick of a fever, in which, being a young man and a soldier too, he could not confine himself to so exact a diet as was necessary. Having spied opportunity that his physician Glaucus was gone unto the theatre to see the sports and pastimes, he went to dinner, and ate a roasted **capon** whole, and drank a great potful of wine, which he had caused to be set in water: whereupon his fever took him so sorely that he lived not long after.

[omission for length: Alexander's grief at the death of his friend]

Now as he was ready to take his journey to go unto **Babylon**, Nearchus his admiral came again unto him from the great Sea Oceanum, by the river of Euphrates, and told him how certain Chaldean soothsayers came unto him, who did warn him that he should not go into Babylon. Howbeit, Alexander made no reckoning of it but went on. But when he came hard to the walls of Babylon, he saw a great number of crows fighting and killing one of another, and some of them fell down dead [near] him. Afterwards it being told him that Apollodorus, the governor of the city of Babylon, having sacrificed unto the gods to know what should happen to him: he sent for the soothsayer Pythagoras, to know of him if it were true. The soothsayer denied it not. Then Alexander asked him what signs he had in the sacrifice. He answered, that the liver was defective in its lobe. "O gods," said Alexander then, "this is an ill sign." Notwithstanding, he did Pythagoras no hurt, but was sorry that he had neglected Nearchus' advice, and stayed for the most part outside the town, removing his tent from place to place, and sailing up and down the Euphrates.

Yet had he many other ill signs and tokens one upon another that made him afraid. For there was a tame ass that killed one of the greatest and goodliest lions in all Babylon with one of his feet. Another time Alexander had put off his clothes, to be anointed to play at **tennis**.

When he should put on his apparel again, the young gentleman that played with him found a man clad in the king's robes, with a **diadem** upon his head, sitting silently upon his throne. Then they asked him what he was? It was long before he made them answer, but at the length coming to himself, he said his name was Dionysius, born in Messina: and being accused for certain crimes committed, he was sent from the sea thither, where he had been a long time prisoner, and also that the god Serapis had appeared unto him, and undone his **irons**, and that he commanded him to take the king's gown and his diadem, and to sit him down in his chair of estate, and say never a word. When Alexander heard it, he put him to death according to the counsel of his soothsayers: but then his mind was troubled. He feared that the gods had forsaken him, and he also grew to suspect his friends.

But first of all, Alexander feared Antipater and his sons, above all other. For one of them called **Iolaus**, was his first cupbearer: and his brother called **Cassander**, was newly come out of Greece unto him. The first time that Cassander saw some of the barbarous people reverencing Alexander, he having been brought up with the manners of Greece, and had never seen the like before: he fell into a loud laughing, very unreverently. Therewith King Alexander was so offended, that he took him by the hair of his head with both his hands and knocked his head and the wall together.

Another time also when Cassander did answer some that accused his father Antipater: King Alexander took him up sharply and said unto him: "What sayest thou?" said he. "Dost thou think that these men would have gone on so long a journey as this, falsely to accuse thy father, if he had not done them wrong?" Cassander again replied unto Alexander, and said, that that was a manifest proof of their false accusation, for that they did now accuse him being so far off, because they thought they could not suddenly be disproved. Alexander smiled, and said, "Lo, these are **Aristotle's quiddities to argue pro and contra**: but this will not save you from punishment, if I find that you have done these men wrong."

In fine, they report that Cassander took such an inward fear and conceit upon it, that long time after when he was king of Macedon, and had all Greece at his commandment: going up and down the city of Delphi, and beholding the monuments and images that are there, he found one of Alexander, which put him into such a sudden fear that the hairs of his head stood upright, and his body quaked in such sort, that it was a great time before he could come to himself again.

Narration and Discussion

Why did the successful training of the Persian boys create such jealousy among the Macedonians?

Did Alexander seem particularly worried by the string of "bad omens?"

For older students: "They answered him, that so doing he should do them great wrong, to send these poor men from him…" Why were Alexander's soldiers so angry with him for suggesting what might seem a humane gesture, sending the wounded away to recover? How can "helping" sometimes be misapplied or misunderstood?

Lesson Twenty-Four

Introduction

This lesson describes the sudden and final illness of Alexander, at the age of thirty-two. The cause of his death has been attributed to everything from alcohol to typhoid fever to poison; but it seems to be a mystery that will never be solved.

Vocabulary

an ague: a fever

all at a draught: in one gulp

fell a-raving: became delirious

the thirtieth day: Plutarch's dates do not match those stated elsewhere, and seem inconsistent even within the text

watch and ward without: keep guard outside

Historic Occasions

323 B.C.: Death of Alexander in Babylon

Reading

Part One

When once Alexander had given way to fears of supernatural influence, his mind was so troubled and afraid, that no strange thing happened unto him, how little soever it was, but he took it straight for a sign and prediction from the gods: so that his tent was always full of priests and soothsayers *[omission]*. So horrible a thing is the mistrust and contempt of the gods, when it is begotten in the hearts of men, and superstition also so dreadful, that it filleth the guilty consciences and fearful hearts like water distilling from above: as at that time it filled Alexander with all folly, after that fear had once possessed him.

This notwithstanding, after that he had received some answers touching Hephaestion from the oracle of Jupiter Ammon, he left his sorrow, and returned again to his banquets and feasting. For he did sumptuously feast Nearchus, and one day when he came out of his bath according to his manner, being ready to go to bed, Medius (one of his captains) besought him to come to a banquet to him at his lodging. Alexander went thither and drank there all that night and the next day, so that he got **an ague** by it. But that came not (as some write) by drinking up Hercules' cup **all at a draught**: neither for the sudden pain he felt between his shoulders, as if he had been thrust into the back with a spear. For all these were thought to be written, by some, for lies and fables, because they would have made the end of this great tragedy lamentable and pitiful. But Aristobulus writeth, that he had such an extreme fever and thirst withal, that he drank wine, and after that **fell a-raving**, and at the length died **the thirtieth day** of the month of June.

[These are the details of his illness.] In his household book of things passed daily, it is written, that his fever being upon him, he slept in his hothouse *[Dryden: in the bathing-room]* on the eighteenth day of June. The next morning after he was come out of his hothouse, he went into his chamber, and passed all that day playing at dice: and at night very late,

114

after he had bathed himself and sacrificed unto the gods, he fell to meat, and had his fever that night. And the twentieth day also, bathing himself again, and making his ordinary sacrifice to the gods, [he lay in the bathing-room], harkening unto Nearchus that told him strange things he had seen in the great Sea Oceanum. The twenty-first day also, having done the like as before, he was much more inflamed then he had been, and felt himself very ill all night, and the next day following in a great fever: and on that day he made his bed to be removed, and to be set up by the fish ponds *[Dryden: by the great bath]*, where he discoursed with his principal officers about finding fit men to fill up the vacant places in the army.

The twenty-third day *[Dryden: the twenty-fourth]*, having an extreme fever upon him, he was carried unto the sacrifices, and commanded that his chiefest captains only should remain in his lodging, and that the other meaner sort should **watch and ward without**. The twenty-fourth day *[Dryden: the twenty-fifth]*, he was carried unto the other palace of the kings, which is on the other side of the lake, where he slept a little, but the fever never left him: and when his captains and noblemen came to do him humble reverence and to see him, he lay speechless.

So did he the following day also: insomuch as the Macedonians thought he was dead. Then they came and knocked at the palace gate, and cried out unto his friends and familiars, and threatened them, so that they were compelled to open them the gate. Thereupon the gates were opened, and they, coming in their gowns, went unto his bedside to see him. That same day Python and Seleucus were appointed by the king's friends to go to the temple of the god Serapis, to know if they should bring King Alexander thither. The god answered them, that they should not remove him from thence.

The eight and twentieth day at night Alexander died. Thus it is written word for word in manner, in the household book of remembrance.

Part Two

At [that] time, there was no suspicion that he was poisoned. Yet they say that, six years after, there appeared some proof that he was poisoned. Whereupon his mother Olympias put many men to death, and cast the ashes of Iolaus into the wind, that was dead before, for that it was said he [Iolaus] gave him [Alexander] poison in his drink.

They that think it was Aristotle that counselled Antipater to do it, by whose means the poison was brought: they say that Hagnothemis reported it, having heard it of King Antigonus' own mouth. The poison (as some say) was cold as ice, and falleth from a rock in the territory of the city of Nonacris, which they gathered like a thin dew, and kept in an ass's hoof; for it was so very cold and penetrating that no other vessel would hold it. Others defend it, and say, that the report of his poisoning is untrue: and for proof thereof they allege this reason, which is of no small importance: that is that the chiefest captains fell at great variance after his death, so that the corpse of Alexander remained many days naked without burial, in a hot dry country, and yet there never appeared any sign or token upon his body that he was poisoned, but it was still a clean and fair corpse as could be.

Roxane, who was now with child, and upon that account much honoured by the Macedonians, did malice Statira extremely, and did finely deceive her by a counterfeit letter she sent, as if it had come from Alexander, willing her to come unto him. But when she was come, Roxane killed her and her sister, and then threw their bodies into a well, and filled it up with earth, with Perdiccas' help and consent.

Perdiccas, in the time immediately following the king's death, under cover of the name of Arrhidaeus, whom he carried about him as a sort of guard to his person, exercised the chief authority [in Macedon].

[brief omission]

Narration and Discussion

In the introductory notes for this study, a teacher describes Alexander's "wisdom, valour, and self-reliance," and his "love of simplicity, generosity, and kindness to his men." Did those traits accurately describe Alexander throughout his life; or did his values change along with events and circumstances?

Creative narration: Take the part of a detective, and explain the motives of the suspects in Alexander's death. Is there enough evidence to make an arrest?

Examination Questions for Term Two

Younger students

1. Why and how did Alexander teach his men to "acquaint themselves with hardness?"

2. How did Alexander go to war with King Porus? Give the whole story.

Older students (Choose two of these)

1. On what occasions were the following words used? Tell the whole story in two cases. (a) "If I drink alone, all these men will faint." (b) "Antipater," he said, "does not know that one tear of a mother effaces a thousand such letters as these."

2. How did Alexander talk with the philosophers of India?

3. "To live at pleasure is a vile thing, and to travail is princely." Why did Alexander thus rebuke his friends? Tell the whole story.

Timoleon
(ca. 411-337 B.C.)

Introduction

Timoleon was a Corinthian citizen who had given up public life after painful personal losses. Nevertheless, when the city needed someone to lead a military mission, he was the top choice. At first he refused, but he was exhorted (or blackmailed) into taking up the challenge; and from that time on, Timoleon became famous "not only for virtues, but for success."

Timoleon's Good Fortune

It is no accident that Plutarch speaks of Fortune as if she were a character in the story. Fortune (or Fortuna) was a Roman deity, the daughter of Jupiter; her Greek equivalent was Tyche. A modern-day derivative might be "Lady Luck." Fortune did not equal random chance, however; her blessings were believed to be tied to one's virtue.

Was Timoleon married?

We are told in **Lesson Eleven** that he had a wife and children, and that he sent for them when he eventually settled in Sicily; but there is no more information than that.

What was Corinth?

Many students will already recognize the city of Corinth, but if not, you will want to find it on a map. Corinth was one of the largest and most important city-states in Ancient Greece. St. Paul wrote two letters to the church in Corinth, about four hundred years after the events described here.

What was Syracuse?

The city-state of Syracuse was located on the island of **Sicily**, which is across the **Strait of Messina** from the mainland city of **Rhegium** (now Reggio Calabria) on the "toe" of Italy's "boot." **Syracuse** was/is in the southeastern corner of the island.

We now associate Sicily with Italy rather than Greece, but Syracuse was a Greek city, founded by the city of Corinth and also allied with Sparta. It was divided into "quarters," or neighbourhoods, including Acradina, Ortygia (or Ortigia), and Epipoli (Epipolae). (See the **Top Vocabulary Terms** note for **castle**.)

Syracuse was ruled by **tyrant** kings (see below), including the cruel Dionysius the Elder, and then his son, Dionysius the Younger (referred to here as **Dionysius**). To make things even more confusing, Dionysius had been sent into exile by his former mentor **Dion** (see Plutarch's *Life of Dion*); but he had ousted Dion and returned to power himself three years later. A weak ruler over an unhappy colony made Syracuse ripe for attack by other powers, such as **Hicetas of Leontini** and the **Carthaginians**.

What is a tyrant?

The idea of a "tyrant king" in the ancient world was somewhat different from the way we use the word today. "Tyrant" meant an absolute ruler, but it wasn't a judgment about whether he was good or evil. In this case, though, the "tyrants" had gone too far; so the Corinthians were asked to restore law and liberty to the colony.

What was Carthage?

Across the **Mediterranean Sea** (in present-day Tunisia) was **Carthage**, a powerful city of the **Phoenicians.** There were also Carthaginian colonies in Sicily, such as **Lilybaeum.**

The Syracusans' fear of the Carthaginians was, apparently, what kept them from rebelling against Dionysius, and also what motivated them to pay high taxes and to volunteer their time building strong walls and war machinery.

What were Leontini and Catana?

The city of **Leontini** was not considered part of Syracuse but was subject to its rule. Its tyrant-king at the time was **Hicetas.** Another city of interest is **Catana** (also Catina or Catania), at the foot of **Mount Etna**, which was ruled by **Mamercus.**

Top Vocabulary Terms in *Timoleon*

If you recognize these words, you are well on your way to mastering the vocabulary of this study. (They will not be noted in the lessons.)

1. **barbarians:** In *Timoleon*, "barbarians" can refer to either foreigners living in Syracuse, or (more often) the Carthaginian enemies. The word does not refer to their morals or manners, but simply their non-Greekness.

2. **buckler:** shield, in Dryden's translation. North prefers **target**.

3. **castle, citadel:** fort. **Ortygia**, an island just across from the rest of the city, was a natural fortress, and had been the original site of Syracuse. Another "castle" was the **Euryalus Fortress**, which was built on a hill called **Epipolae.**

4. **corn:** grain, usually wheat or barley

5. **footmen:** foot soldiers, infantry, sometimes called "foot." **Horsemen** are the cavalry, or simply "horse."

120

6. **galley:** a ship powered both by sails and by banks of oars

7. **mercenary:** Mercenary soldiers are those hired to fight for pay, who do not have a personal interest in the outcome. **"Soldiers who were strangers"** also refers to mercenaries.

8. **stay:** Often used to mean delay, detain, stop. It can also be used in the more familiar sense of "remain" (stay here).

9. **victuals** (pronounced "vittles"): food. A **victualler** is a food supplier or grocer. **Provisions** are food and other necessary supplies.

Lesson One

Introduction

Like Shakespeare writing a play, Plutarch begins the *Life of Timoleon* by setting the stage and introducing supporting characters. **Lesson One** shows why a main character exactly like Timoleon was badly needed. But Timoleon himself does not come onstage until **Lesson Two**.

Vocabulary

ignoble, base, or vicious: unworthy, evil

good fortune: see introductory note about Fortune

before Timoleon was sent into Sicily: this is the main event of the story, but we are not going to hear about that quite yet

in this posture: like this

train of mischiefs: string of unhappy events

tyrant: see introductory note

dogged: relentless

sanctuary: place of safety

an embassy: ambassadors, representatives

confided in: trusted

commended the design: praised the intentions

People

Paulus Aemilius: a Roman statesman whose story Plutarch chose to be a "parallel life" with that of Timoleon

Dion, Dionysius I, Dionysius II, etc.: see introductory notes

Hicetas: A tyrant ruler (see introductory notes). Dryden spells his name **Hicetes**, but North uses **Hicetas**, and that seems to be the common spelling today.

Historic Occasions

411 B.C.: Birth of Timoleon (approximate)

409 B.C.: War against **Carthage** (see introductory notes)

c. 397 B.C.: Birth of Dionysius II

367 B.C.: Death of Dionysius I

366 B.C.: Dionysius II took full control over Syracuse

365 B.C. (approximately): Death of Timoleon's brother (the cause of his withdrawal from public life)

357 B.C.: Dionysius II deposed by Dion

354 B.C.: Dion killed and Dionysius II returned to power

344 B.C.: Syracuse appealed to Corinth for aid

On the Map

On a map (preferably one showing this period in history), locate the

Mediterranean Sea, the Ionian Sea, mainland Italy, Sicily, Syracuse, Carthage, Greece, Corinth. (Or label them on a blank map.)

Peloponnesus: the southern half of Greece

Reading

Prologue

It was for the sake of others that I first commenced writing biographies; but I find myself proceeding and attaching myself to it for my own; the virtues of these great men serving me as a sort of looking-glass, in which I may see how to adjust and adorn my own life. Indeed, it can be compared to nothing but daily living and associating together; we receive, as it were, in our inquiry, and entertain each successive guest, view—

Their stature and their qualities,

and select from their actions all that is noblest and worthiest to know.

"Ah, and what greater pleasure can one have?"

...or what more effective means to one's moral improvement?

[omission]

My method is, by the study of history, and by the familiarity acquired in writing, to habituate my memory to receive and retain images of the best and worthiest characters. I thus am enabled to free myself from any **ignoble, base, or vicious** impressions, contracted from the contagion of ill company that I may be unavoidably engaged in; by the remedy of turning my thoughts in a happy and calm temper to view these noble examples. Of this kind are those of Timoleon the Corinthian and **Paulus Aemilius**, to write whose lives is my present business: men equally famous, not only for their virtues, but success; insomuch that they have left it doubtful whether they owe their greatest achievements to **good fortune**, or their own prudence and conduct.

Part One

The affairs of the **Syracusans, before Timoleon was sent into Sicily,** were **in this posture:** after **Dion** had driven out the tyrant **Dionysius I,** he himself was slain by treachery; and thus the city by a continual change of governors, and a **train of mischiefs** that succeeded each other, became almost abandoned; while of the rest of Sicily, part was now utterly depopulated and desolate through long continuance of war, and most of the cities that had been left standing were in the hands of **barbarians** and soldiers out of employment, that were ready to embrace every turn of government.

Such being the state of things, **Dionysius II** [took] the opportunity, and in the tenth year of his banishment, by the help of some mercenary troops he had got together, [forced out the temporary ruler of Syracuse]; [recovered] all afresh; and again settled in his dominion. So, if he was strangely expulsed by a small power out of the greatest kingdom that ever was in the world: likewise he more strangely recovered it again, being banished and very poor, making himself king over them who before had driven him out. Thus were the inhabitants of the city compelled to serve this **tyrant:** who besides [the fact] that of his own nature he was never courteous nor civil, he was now grown to be far more **dogged** and cruel, by reason of the extreme misery and misfortune he had endured.

The better and more distinguished citizens [had gone] to Hicetas, ruler of the Leontines, put themselves under his protection, and chose him for their general in the war; not that he was much preferable to any open and avowed tyrant, but they had no other **sanctuary** at present, and it gave them some ground of confidence that he was of a Syracusan family, and had forces able to encounter those of Dionysius.

Part Two

In the meantime the Carthaginians appeared before Sicily with a great navy, watching when and where they might make a descent upon the island; and terror at this fleet made the Sicilians incline to send **an embassy** into Greece, to pray aid from the Corinthians, whom they **confided in** rather than others, not only upon the account of their near kindred, and the great benefits they had often received by trusting them, but but also for that they knew that Corinth was a city that, in all ages and times, did ever love liberty and hate tyrants, and that had always made their greatest wars not for ambition of kingdoms, nor of covetous desire to conquer and rule, but only to defend and maintain the liberty of the Greeks.

But Hicetas, who made it the business of his command not so much to deliver the Syracusans from other tyrants as to enslave them to himself, had already entered into some secret conferences with those of Carthage, while in public he **commended the design** of his Syracusan clients, and despatched ambassadors from himself, together with theirs, into **Peloponnesus**; not that he really desired any relief to come from there, but in case the Corinthians, as was likely enough, on account of the troubles of Greece and occupation at home, should refuse their assistance, hoping then he should be able with less difficulty to dispose and incline things for the Carthaginian interest, and so make use of these foreign pretenders, as instruments and auxiliaries for himself, either against the Syracusans or Dionysius, as occasion served. And that this was his full purpose, and intent, it appeared plainly soon after.

Narration and Discussion

Why did the Syracusans agree to seek help from the Corinthians?

Why was King Hicetas so eager to send his ambassadors to Corinth?

For further thought: Plutarch says that writing about the lives of great men is "a sort of looking-glass, in which I may see how to adjust and adorn my own life." Do you find that reading biographies gives you that same advantage?

For older students: Plutarch describes Corinth as a place governed "not for ambition of kingdoms, nor of covetous desire to conquer and rule, but only to defend and maintain the liberty of the Grecians" (North's translation). Some people might argue that any government will take from rather than support its citizens, because "power corrupts." Do you believe that a government (of a city or a country) can be an example of integrity to its own people and to others?

Creative narration: To help with both readings and narrations, it would be useful to set up a tabletop model showing key locations (perhaps drawn on large sheets of paper): Syracuse and Carthage (with the Strait of Sicily between them), and (somewhere further away) Corinth. The characters don't have to be realistic: toy figures or toothpicks with nametags attached will work. Toy ships or buildings can be put to use, but materials such as construction bricks, natural materials, or household objects are fine too (a box could represent the Syracusan "castle").

What action might be shown for **Lesson One**? Suggestions: the appearance of the Carthaginian navy; the reaction of the Syracusans.

Lesson Two

Introduction

In this lesson we hear about the worst time in the life of Timoleon, caused by the love and loyalty he felt towards his "rash, hair-brained" brother. How far would he go to cover up Timophanes' errors, and excuse his selfishness?

Vocabulary

sought unto them: asked them for help

magistrates: rulers

various aspirants for reputation: various people who were qualified to lead the expedition

mean: lowly

Fortune: see introductory note

prudence: caution, restraint

rash, hairbrained: unwise and impulsive

bare him in hand: made him behave

salve: mend, soothe

sported: laughed, mocked

waxed warm: got heated up

murder he had committed: Timoleon did not kill Timophanes by his own hand, but he was held responsible for his death

disconsolate: sad, inconsolable

People

Aeschylus, Satyrus: men involved in the death of Timophanes

Historic Occasions

365 B.C. (approximately): Death of Timophanes

On the Map

Aegina (Aeginetes): a Greek island near Athens

Argos: a city in Argolis, in the Peloponnesus

Cleonae: a city located on the road from Argos to Corinth

Zacynthe [Zakynthos]: an island off the west coast of Greece

Iapygia (Iapygians): also called Apulia; the region of Italy which occupies the heel of Italy's "boot"

Pachynus: now called Capo Passero or Passaro, on the southeastern side of Sicily

Libya: a country of northern Africa, on the Mediterranean Sea

Great Syrtis: the Gulf of Sidra, on the northern coast of Libya

Minoa: Heraclea Minoa, a city on the south coast of Sicily

Reading

Prologue

Now when the Syracusan ambassadors arrived at Corinth, and had delivered their message, the Corinthians, who had ever been careful to defend such cities as had **sought unto them**, and specially Syracuse, since by good fortune there was nothing to molest them in their own country, where they were enjoying peace and leisure at that time, they readily and with one accord passed a vote for their assistance. And when they were deliberating about the choice of a captain for the expedition, and the **magistrates** were urging the claims of **various aspirants for reputation**, one of the crowd stood up and named Timoleon, son of Timodemus, who had long absented himself from public business, and had neither any thoughts of, nor the least pretensions to, an employment of that nature.

And truly it is to be thought it was the secret working of the gods that directed the thought of this **mean** commoner to name Timoleon: whose election **Fortune** favoured very much, and who joined to his valiantness and virtue marvellous good success in all his doings afterwards.

Part One (a flashback)

This Timoleon was born of noble parents, both by father and mother: his father was called Timodemus, and his mother Demariste; and as for himself, he was noted for his love of his country, and his gentleness of temper, except in his extreme hatred to tyrants and wicked men. His natural abilities for war were so happily tempered, that while a rare **prudence** might be seen in all the enterprises of his younger years, an equal courage showed itself in the last exploits of his declining age.

He had an elder brother called **Timophanes**, who was nothing like to him in condition: for he was a **rash, hairbrained** man, and had a greedy desire to reign, it being put into his head by a company of mean men that **bare him in hand** they were his friends; and by certain soldiers gathered together which he had always about him. And because he was very hot and forward in wars, his citizens took him for a noble captain, and a man of good service, and therefore oftentimes they gave him charge of men. And therein Timoleon did help him much to hide his fault he committed, or at the least made them seem less, and lighter than they were, still increasing that small good gift that nature brought forth in Timophanes.

It happened once in the battle fought by the Corinthians against the forces of **Argos** and **Cleonae**, that Timoleon served among the infantry, when Timophanes, commanding their cavalry, was brought into extreme danger; as his horse, being hurt, threw him on the ground in the midst of his enemies, while part of his companions dispersed at once in a panic, and the small number that remained, bearing up against a great multitude, had much ado to maintain any resistance. As soon, therefore, as Timoleon was aware of the accident, he ran hastily in to his brother's rescue, and covering the fallen Timophanes with his buckler, after having received abundance of darts, and several strokes by the sword upon his body and his armour, he at length with much difficulty obliged the enemies to retire, and brought off his brother alive and safe.

But the Corinthians, for fear of losing their city a second time, as they had once before, by admitting their allies, made a decree to maintain four hundred mercenaries for its security, and gave Timophanes the command over them. He, abandoning all honesty and regard of the trust the Corinthians reposed in him, [attempted] all the ways he could to make himself lord of the city; and having put many of the chiefest citizens to death without order of law, in the end he openly proclaimed himself king of Corinth.

Timoleon being very sorry for this and thinking his brother's wickedness would be the very highway to his fall and destruction, sought first to win him with all the good words and persuasion he could, to move him to leave his ambitious desire to reign, and to **salve** (as near as might be) his hard dealing with the citizens. Timophanes would give no ear unto his brother's persuasions.

Thereupon Timoleon then went unto one **Aeschylus**, his friend (and brother unto Timophanes' wife), and to one **Satyrus**, a soothsayer (as Theopompus the historiographer calleth him, and Ephorus calleth him Orthagoras). With them he came again another time unto his brother; and they three coming to him, instantly besought him to believe good counsel, and to leave the kingdom. Timophanes at the first did but laugh them to scorn, and he **sported** at their persuasions;

129

but afterwards he **waxed warm** and grew into great **choler** with them. Timoleon, seeing that, went a little aside, and, covering his face, fell a-weeping: and the other two drawing out their swords, they slew Timophanes in the place.

Part Two (the flashback continues)

This was straight blown abroad through the city, and the better sort did greatly commend the noble mind and hatred of wrong that Timoleon bare against the tyrant: considering that he being of a gentle nature, and loving to his kin, did notwithstanding regard the benefit of his country before the natural affection to his brother, and preferred duty and justice before nature and kindred.

For before, he had saved his brother's life, fighting for defense of his country; and now in Timophanes' seeking to make himself king, and to rule the same, he made him to be slain. Such people then as misliked popular government and liberty, and always followed the nobility, they set a good face of the matter, as though they had been glad of the tyrant's death. Yet still reproving Timoleon for the horrible **murder he had committed** against his brother, declaring how detestable it was both to the gods and men: they so handled him, that it grieved him to the heart he had done it. But when it was told him that his mother took it marvellous evil, and that she pronounced horrible curses against him, and gave out terrible words of him, he went unto her in hope to comfort her: howbeit she could never abide to see him, but always shut her door against him.

With grief at this he grew so disordered in his mind and so **disconsolate**, that he determined to put an end to his perplexity with his life, by abstaining from all food. But through the care and diligence of his friends, who were every instant with him, and added force to their entreaties, he came to resolve and promise at last, that he would endure living, provided it might be in solitude, and remote from company; so that, quitting all civil transactions and commerce with the world for a long while after his first retirement, he never came into Corinth, but wandered up and down the fields, full of anxious and tormenting thoughts, and spent his time in desert places, at the farthest distance from society and human interaction.

So true it is that the minds of men are easily shaken and carried off from their own sentiments through the casual commendation or reproof of others, unless the judgments that we make, and the purposes we conceive, be confirmed by reason and philosophy, and thus obtain strength and steadiness. An action must not only be just and laudable in its own nature, but it must proceed likewise from solid motives and a lasting principle, that so we may fully and constantly approve the thing, and be perfectly satisfied in what we do; for otherwise, after having put our resolution into practice, we shall out of pure weakness come to be troubled at the performance, when the grace and godliness, which rendered it before so amiable and pleasing to us, begin to decay and wear out of our fancy; like greedy people, who, seizing on the more delicious morsels of any dish with a keen appetite, are presently disgusted when they grow full, and find themselves oppressed and uneasy now by what they before so greedily desired.

[omission for length and mature content]

Narration and Discussion

How did Timoleon show much love, but perhaps not enough wisdom, in dealing with his brother's weaknesses?

"And thus we see that counsels and judgments are lightly carried away (by praise or dispraise) if they be not shored up with rule of reason and philosophy, and [thus obtain strength and steadiness]." Why should we avoid putting too much importance on others' praise or criticism? Compare Proverbs 12:15 with Prov. 17:4.

For older students: Those who have read about the assassination of Julius Caesar might compare it with the death of Timophanes. ("Not that I loved Caesar less, but that I loved Rome more.") How might this experience have coloured Timoleon's feelings about the later call for him to fight against tyranny?

Creative narration #1: Use the model you created earlier to help retell this lesson. Note that most of the action in **Lesson Two** takes place in Corinth rather than Syracuse.

Creative narration #2: Dramatize part of this story, e.g. the reaction of the Corinthians to the Syracusan ambassadors' request for help, and the suggestion that they call on Timoleon to help rescue the colony. Do you think they would expect him to say yes? Imagine a conversation between those who remember the story of Timoleon, and those who need to be filled in on the details.

Lesson Three

Introduction

As the Corinthians prepared to sail to Syracuse, letters arrived from the tyrant Hicetas, trying to persuade them that their help was not needed, and pointing out that they could not be successful against the Carthaginians, so they would be putting themselves into needless danger by even attempting this intervention. However, this attempt at discouragement backfired, and even those who had been unsure about the mission were now convinced that it was the right thing to do.

Vocabulary

suffrages: votes, voices

two faces in one hood: two-faced, or double-dealing

made league and amity: made an alliance

supply Timoleon: supply him with soldiers, weapons, etc.

Proserpina: Proserpina is the Roman name for Persephone, a goddess who, along with her mother **Ceres** (or Demeter) was worshipped throughout Greece.

Apollo: a major god in both Greek and Roman mythology

riband: decorative ribbon

prosperous gale: strong wind

mysteries: religious rituals

soothsayers: those who read religious omens

reduced: taken over, captured

quarters: neighbourhoods, boroughs

recompense: payment

People

Dionysius: see introductory notes

Historic Occasions

344 B.C.: Campaign to restore liberty to Syracuse

On the Map

Delphi: a sacred place where, it was believed, one could receive prophecies and the answers to troubling questions

Corcyra (Corfu): an island in the Ionian Sea; also the principal city on that island

Leucadia (Lefkada): an island in the Ionian Sea; also the city by that name

Rhegium (Reggio di Calabria): a Greek city located on the toe of Italy's "boot," directly across from Sicily. St. Paul's ship made a stop at Rhegium when he was being taken to Rome (Acts 28:13).

Reading

Part One

The grief of Timoleon at what had been done, whether it arose from **commiseration** of his brother's fate, or the reverence he bore his mother, so shattered and broke his spirits that for the space of almost twenty years he had not offered to concern himself in any honourable or public action. When, therefore, he was pitched upon for a general, and, joyfully, accepted as such by the **suffrages** of the people, Teleclides, who was at that time the most powerful and distinguished man in Corinth, began to exhort him that he would act now like a man of worth and gallantry: "For," said he, "if you do bravely in this service we shall believe that you delivered us from a tyrant; but if otherwise that you killed your brother."

While Timoleon was yet preparing to set sail, and enlisting soldiers to embark with him, letters came to the Corinthians from Hicetas, whereby it plainly appeared that Hicetas had carried **two faces in one hood**, and that he was become a traitor. For he had no sooner dispatched his ambassadors unto them, but he straight took the Carthaginians' part, and dealt openly for them, intending to drive out Dionysius and to make himself king of Syracuse. But fearing lest the Corinthians would send aid before this were effected, he wrote again unto the Corinthians, sending them word that they should not need now to put themselves to any charge or danger for coming into Sicily, and specially because the Carthaginians were very angry, and did also lie in wait in the way as they should come, with a great fleet of ships to meet with their army: and that for himself, because he saw they tarried long, he had **made league and amity** with the Carthaginians against the tyrant Dionysius.

This letter being publicly read, if any had been cold and indifferent before as to the expedition in hand, the indignation they now conceived against Hicetas so exasperated and inflamed them all that they willingly contributed to **supply Timoleon**, and endeavoured with one accord to hasten his departure.

Part Two

When the vessels were equipped, and the soldiers every way provided for, the female priest of **Proserpina** had a dream or vision wherein the goddesses **Ceres** and Proserpina did appear, appareled like travelers to take a journey, and were heard to say that they were going to sail with Timoleon into Sicily; whereupon the Corinthians, having built a sacred galley, devoted it to them, and called it the Galley of the Goddesses.

Timoleon went in person to **Delphi**, where he sacrificed to **Apollo**, and, descending into the place of prophecy, was surprised with the following marvellous occurrence. A **riband**, with crowns and figures of victory embroidered upon it, slipped off from among the gifts that were there consecrated and hung up in the temple, and fell down directly upon his head, so that Apollo seemed already to crown him with success, and send him thence to conquer and triumph.

He took ship and sailed with seven galleys of Corinth, two of **Corcyra**, and a tenth which was furnished by the **Leucadians**; and when he was now entered into the deep by night, and carried with a **prosperous gale**, the heaven seemed all on a sudden to break open, and a bright spreading flame to issue forth from it, and hover over the ship he was in; and, having formed itself into a torch, not unlike those that are used in the **mysteries**, it began to steer the same course, and run along in their company, guiding them by its light to that quarter of Italy where they designed to go ashore. The **soothsayers** affirmed that this apparition agreed with the dream of the holy woman, since the goddesses were now visibly joining in the expedition, and sending this light from heaven before them, Sicily being thought sacred to Proserpina.

[short omission]

These early demonstrations of divine favour greatly encouraged his whole army; so that, making all the speed they were able, by a voyage across the open sea, they were soon passing along the coast of Italy.

Part Three

But when they came thither, the news they understood from Sicily put Timoleon in great perplexity, and did marvellously discourage the soldiers he brought with him.

For Hicetas, having already beaten Dionysius out of the field, and **reduced** most of the **quarters** of Syracuse itself, now hemmed him in and besieged him in the citadel and what is called the Island, whither he was fled for his last refuge; while the Carthaginians, by agreement, were to make it their business to hinder Timoleon from landing in any port of Sicily; so that he and his party being driven back, they might with ease and at their own leisure divide the island among themselves.

The Carthaginians, following his request, sent twenty of their galleys unto **Rhegium**, among which Hicetas' ambassadors were sent to Timoleon, with testimony of his doings: for they were fair flattering words, to cloak the wicked intent he purposed. For they willed Timoleon he should go himself alone ("if he thought good") unto Hicetas, to counsel him, and to accompany him in all his doings, which were now so far onwards as he had almost ended them all. Furthermore, they did also persuade him that he should send back his ships and soldiers to Corinth again, considering that the war was now brought to good pass, and the Carthaginians had blocked up the passage, determined to oppose them if they should try to force their way towards the shore.

So the Corinthians, at their arrival into the city of Rhegium, finding there these ambassadors, and seeing the fleet of the Carthaginians' ships, which did ride at anchor not far off from them: it spited them on the one side to see they were thus mocked and abused by Hicetas. For every one of them were marvellous angry with him, and were greatly afeared also for the poor Sicilians, whom too plainly they saw were left a prey unto Hicetas for reward of his treason, and to the Carthaginians for **recompense** of the tyranny which they suffered him to establish. For it seemed utterly impossible to force and overbear the Carthaginian ships that lay before them and were double their number, as also to vanquish the victorious troops which Hicetas had with him in Syracuse, to take the lead of which very troops they had undertaken their voyage.

Narration and Discussion

How was Timoleon convinced to accept the mission to Syracuse?

Why was there such "perplexity" over the situation (in Part Three)?

Creative narration #1: Use the model to show the action of this lesson.

Creative narration #2: Dramatize a meeting to discuss the current situation; or describe it in a news report, letter, or journal entry.

Lesson Four

Introduction

Timoleon appeared to be surrendering to the demands of Hicetas; but through a clever trick, he managed to escape from Rhegium and cross over to Sicily. To his surprise, many of the Sicilian towns were mistrustful of even Corinthian help, and offered no co-operation. One city, Adranum, did want help against Dionysius, but the people were divided on which army to ask, so they invited everybody at once. On the way there, Timoleon's army ambushed Hicetas and his troops, and that victory brought them the full support of Adranum.

Vocabulary

compliance: co-operation, obedience

conduce to his own security and discharge: protect him and help him to carry out the task

obliged: committed, bound

the barbarous people; the Phoenicians: the Carthaginians

haven: harbour

an oration: a speech

about the hustings: around the platform

bore sway: had control

muster up his troops: gather his soldiers

confide: trust

expired in servitude: died in slavery

specious pretenses: misleading statements; false promises

dissension: conflict

three hundred and forty furlongs: about 42 miles (68 km)

the vanguard: those at the front

thirty furlongs: about 3.75 miles (6 km)

javelin: a long, pointed weapon; spear

People

Andromachus: the ruler of **Tauromenium**

On the Map

Adranum, Tauromenium: cities on the east coast of Sicily

Reading

Part One

The case being thus, Timoleon, after some conference with the envoys of Hicetas and the Carthaginian captains, told them he should readily submit to their proposals: to what purpose would it be to refuse **compliance**? He was desirous only, before his return to Corinth, that what had passed between them in private might be solemnly declared before the people of Rhegium, a Greek city and a common friend to the parties. This, he said, would very much **conduce to his own security and discharge**; and they likewise would more strictly observe articles of agreement, on behalf of the Syracusans, which they had **obliged** themselves to in the presence of so many witnesses. The design of all this was only to divert their attention, while he got an opportunity of slipping away from their fleet; which the captains and governors of Rhegium did favour, and did seem to help him in: because they wished Sicily should fall into the hands of the Corinthians, and they feared much to have **the barbarous people** for their neighbours.

For this cause, they commanded a general assembly of all the people, during which time they caused the gates of the city to be shut: giving it out that it was because the citizens should not go about any other matters in the meantime. A succession of speakers came forward, addressing the people at great length, to the same effect, without bringing the subject to any conclusion, making way each for another and purposely spinning out the time, till the Corinthian galleys should get clear of the **haven**; the Carthaginian commanders being detained there without any suspicion, as also Timoleon still remained present, and gave signs as if he were just preparing to make **an oration**.

But upon secret notice that the rest of the galleys were already gone off, and that his alone remained waiting for him, by the help and concealment of those Rhegians that were **about the hustings** and favoured his departure, he made shift to slip away through the crowd, and running down to the port, set sail with all speed.

Part Two

And when he had overtaken his fleet, they went all safe together to land at the city of **Tauromenium**, which is in Sicily. There they were very well received by **Andromachus**, then ruler of the city. He was the father of Timaeus the historian, and incomparably the best of all those that **bore sway** in Sicily at that time, governing his citizens according to law and justice and openly professing an aversion and enmity to all tyrants; upon which account he gave Timoleon leave to **muster up his troops** there, and to make that city the seat of war, persuading the inhabitants to join their arms with the Corinthian forces, and assist them in the design of delivering Sicily from bondage.

But the captains of the Carthaginians that were at Rhegium, when they knew that Timoleon was under sail and gone, after the assembly was broken up: they were ready to eat their fingers for spite, to see themselves thus finely mocked and deceived. The Rhegians, on the other side, were merry at the matter, to see how the **Phoenicians** stormed at having such a fine part played them. However, they despatched a messenger aboard one of their galleys to Tauromenium, who, after much blustering in the insolent barbaric way, and many menaces to Andromachus if he did not forthwith send the Corinthians off, stretched out his hand with the inside upward, and then turning it down again, threatened he would handle their city even so, and turn it topsy-turvy in as little time, and with as much ease. Andromachus fell a-laughing at him, and he did turn his hand up and down as the ambassador had done, and bid him hasten his own departure, unless he had a mind to see that kind of dexterity practiced first upon the galley which brought him hither.

Part Three

Hicetas was informed that Timoleon had landed in Sicily, and, being afraid, sent for a great number of galleys from the Carthaginians. Then the Syracusans began to despair utterly when they saw their haven full of the Carthaginian galleys, the best part of their city kept by Hicetas, and the castle [held] by the tyrant Dionysius. And on the other side, that Timoleon was not yet come but to a little corner of Sicily, having no more but the little city of the Tauromenians, with a small power and less hope: because there were not above a thousand footmen in all to furnish these wars, neither provision of victuals, nor so much money as would serve to entertain and pay them.

Nor did the other towns of Sicily **confide** in him, overpowered as they were with violence and outrage, and embittered against all that should offer to lead armies by the treacherous conduct chiefly of Callipus, an Athenian, and Pharax, a Lacedaemonian captain, both of whom, after giving out that the design of their coming was to introduce liberty and to depose tyrants, [became such tyrants] themselves, that the reign of former oppressors seemed to be a golden age in comparison, and the Sicilians began to consider those more happy who had **expired in servitude**, than any that had lived to see such a dismal freedom.

Looking, therefore, for no better usage from the Corinthian general, but imagining that it was only the same old course of things once more, **specious pretenses** and false professions to allure them by fair hopes and kind promises into the obedience of a new master, they all, with one accord, excepting the people of Adranum, suspected the exhortations, and rejected the overtures that were made them in his name.

The only exception was the city of **Adranum** (consecrated to the god Adranus, and greatly honoured and reverenced through all Sicily); which was then in **dissension**, one person against another, insomuch as one part of them took part with Hicetas and the Carthaginians, and another side of them sent unto Timoleon. It so fell out that these auxiliaries, striving which should be soonest, both arrived at Adranum about the same time.

Part Four

Hicetas brought with him at least five thousand men, while all the force Timoleon could make did not exceed twelve hundred. With these he marched out of **Tauromenium**, which was about **three hundred and forty furlongs** distance from that city. The first day he moved but slowly, and took up his quarters betimes after a short journey; but the day following he quickened his pace, and, having passed through much difficult ground, towards evening received advice that Hicetes was just approaching Adranum, and pitching his camp before it; upon which intelligence, his captains and other officers caused **the vanguard** to halt, that the army being refreshed, and having reposed a while, might engage the enemy with better heart.

But Timoleon, coming up in haste, desired them not to stop for that reason, but rather use all possible diligence to surprise the enemy, whom probably they would now find in disorder, as having lately ended their march and being taken up at present in erecting tents and preparing supper; which he had no sooner said, but laying hold of his buckler and putting himself in the front, he led them on as it were to certain victory. The soldiers, seeing this, followed at his heels with like courage.

They were now within less than **thirty furlongs** of Adranum, which they quickly traversed, and immediately fell in upon the enemy, who were seized with confusion, and began to retire at their first approaches; one consequence of which was that, amidst so little opposition, and so early and general a flight, there were not many more than three hundred slain, and about twice the number made prisoners. Their camp and baggage, however, was all taken.

Then the Adranitans, opening their gates, yielded unto Timoleon, declaring unto him with great fear, and no less wonder, how at the very time when he gave charge upon the enemies, the doors of the temple of their god opened of themselves, and that the **javelin** which the image of their god did hold in his hand, did shake at the very end where the iron head was, and how all his face was seen to sweat.

This (in my opinion) did not only signify the victory he [Timoleon] had gotten at that time, but all the notable exploits he did afterwards, unto the which, this first encounter gave a happy beginning. For immediately after, many cities sent unto Timoleon to join in league with him. And Mamercus the tyrant of Catana, a soldier, and very full of money, did also seek his friendship.

Narration and Discussion

How did Timoleon lead his troops to victory over Hicetas, although they were outnumbered?

Tell all as you can about Andromachus. As a creative narration, you could include opinions and examples of his honesty and good leadership from his friends, servants, etc.

Creative narration #1: Use the model you created earlier to show Timoleon's actions during this lesson. Be sure to mark out a spot for **Adranum**, as it will be needed in future lessons.

Creative narration #2: Those studying in groups might enjoy acting out the assembly scene in Rhegium.

Lesson Five

Introduction

The first part of this lesson describes the surrender of Dionysius to the Corinthians, after the victory over Hicetas. The rest is a sort of sidebar to the main story, telling about the banishment of Dionysius to Corinth, and his activities there (such as having dinner with Philip of Macedon and chatting with Diogenes the philosopher). Dionysius, unfortunately, did not live long after these events.

Vocabulary

baffled: defied, defeated

engines: large devices for attacking, such as catapults

darts: spears

the less regarded: less esteemed (and therefore less of a threat)

feigned: pretended, faked

the many evils attaching to the condition of sovereignty: the hardships of being a king

infelicity: misfortune

when thou goest hence: when you leave

speak in banter: joke around

People

Plato: one of the most famous Greek philosophers. **Dion** had studied with him in Syracuse years before and had brought him to the court again to mentor young **Dionysius**; but things had worked out badly between them.

Philip [the] king of Macedon: the father of Alexander the Great

Diogenes of Sinope: one of the founders of Cynic philosophy.

Philistus/Philistos (432-356 B.C.): a Syracusan historian. The Roman orator Cicero (much later) complimented him by calling him "the miniature Thucydides." It was partly through his wealth and influence that Dionysius I had been able to rise to power in Syracuse.

Historic Occasions

343 B.C.: the surrender (and later the death) of Dionysius

Reading

Part One

Dionysius himself, being now grown desperate, and well-nigh forced to surrender, despising Hicetas who had been thus shamefully **baffled**, and admiring the valour of Timoleon, found means to advertise him and his Corinthians that he [Dionysius] should be content to deliver up himself and the citadel into their hands.

Timoleon, gladly embracing this unlooked-for advantage, sent Euclides and Telemachus, two Corinthian captains, to take possession of the castle, with four hundred men: not all at a time, nor openly (for it was impossible, the enemies lying in wait in the haven); but by small companies, and by stealth, he conveyed them all into the castle. And so they took possession of the fortress and the palace of Dionysius, with all the stores and ammunition he had prepared and laid up to maintain the war. They found a good number of horses, every variety of **engines**, a multitude of **darts**, and weapons that had been gathered together of long time to arm seventy thousand men. Moreover, besides all this, there were two thousand soldiers, whom (with the other things mentioned) Dionysius delivered up into the hands of Timoleon.

Dionysius himself, putting his treasure aboard, and taking a few friends, sailed away unobserved by Hicetas; and being brought to the camp of Timoleon, there first appeared in the humble dress of a private person, and was shortly after sent to Corinth with a single ship and a small sum of money.

Part Two

Dionysius was born and educated in the most splendid court and the most absolute monarchy that ever was, which he held and kept up for the space of ten years succeeding his father's death. He had, after Dion's expedition, spent twelve other years in a continual agitation of wars and contests, and great variety of fortune, during which time all the mischiefs he had committed in his former reign were more than repaid by the ills he himself then suffered *[omission]*; the particulars of which are more exactly given in the *Life of Dion*.

Now when Dionysius was arrived in the city of Corinth, every Grecian was wonderful desirous to go see him, and to talk with him. And some went thither very glad of his overthrow, as if they had trodden him down with their feet, whom fortune had overthrown, so bitterly did they hate him. Others, pitying him in their hearts to see so great a change, did behold him as it were with a certain compassion, considering what great power secret and divine causes have over men's weakness and frailty, and those things that daily passeth over our heads.

For the world then did never bring forth any work of nature or of man's hand so wonderful, as was this of Fortune. Fortune made the world see a man that, before, was in manner lord and king of all Sicily, sit then commonly in the city of Corinth, loitering about perhaps in the fish-market; or sitting a whole day in a perfumer's shop; or commonly drinking in some cellar or tavern; or to brawl and scold in the midst of the streets with common women; or pretending to instruct the singing women of the theatre, and seriously disputing with them about the measure and harmony of pieces of music that were performed there.

Now some say he did this because he knew not else how he should drive the time away, for that indeed he was of a base mind *[omission]*. Other are of opinion that he did it to be **the less regarded**, for fear lest the Corinthians should have him in jealousy and suspicion, imagining that he did take the change and state of his life in grievous part; and that he should yet look back, hoping for a time to recover his state again: and that for this cause he did it, and of purpose **feigned** many things against his nature *[omission]*.

Some notwithstanding have gathered together certain of his answers, which do testify that he did not do all these things of a base brutish mind, but to fit himself only to his present misery and misfortune. For when he came to Leucades, an ancient city built by the Corinthians, as was also the city of Syracuse, he told the inhabitants of the same that he was like to young boys that had done a fault. "For as they flee from their fathers, being ashamed to come in their sight, and are gladder to be with their brethren: even so is it with me," said he, "for it would please me better to dwell here with you, than to go to Corinth, our head city."

Another time, being at Corinth, a stranger *[omission]* asked him, in derision, what benefit he got by **Plato's** wisdom and knowledge. As to the benefit of it, Dionysius answered him again: "How thinkest thou, hath it done good, when thou seest me bear so patiently this change of fortune?" *[Dryden: "Do you think I have made no profit of his philosophy when you see me bear my change of fortune as I do?"]* And when Aristoxenus, the musician, and several others, desired to know how Plato offended him, and what had been the ground of his displeasure with him: he answered that, of **the many evils attaching to the condition of sovereignty**, the one greatest **infelicity** was that none of those who were accounted friends would venture to speak freely, or tell the plain truth; and that by means of such he had been deprived to Plato's kindness.

Another time there cometh a pleasant fellow to him, and, thinking to mock him finely: as he entered into his chamber, he shook his gown, as the manner is when people come to tyrants, to show that they have no weapons under their gowns. But Dionysius encountered him as pleasantly, saying to him: "Do that **when thou goest hence**, to see if thou hast stolen nothing."

And when Philip of Macedon, at a drinking party, began to **speak in banter** about the verses and tragedies which Dionysius his father had made; making as though he wondered at them, how possibly he could have leisure to do them: Dionysius answered him very trimly, and to good purpose. "He did them even at such times," quoth he, "as you and I, and all other great lords whom they reckon happy, are disposed to be drunk, and play the fools." [*Dryden: "It was at those leisurable hours, which such as you and I, and those we call happy men, bestow upon our cups."*]

Plato had not the opportunity to see Dionysius at Corinth, being already dead before he came thither. But **Diogenes of Sinope**, the first time that ever he met with Dionysius, said unto him: "O, how unworthy art thou of this state." Dionysius stayed suddenly, and replied, saying "I thank you, Diogenes, for your condolences." "Condole with you!" replied Diogenes. "Do you not suppose that, on the contrary, I am indignant that such a slave as you, who, if you had your due, should have been let alone to grow old and die in the state of tyranny, as your father did before you, should now enjoy the ease of private persons, and be here to sport and frolic in our society?"

[omission]

Such anecdotes will not, I conceive, be thought either foreign to my purpose of writing *Lives*, or unprofitable in themselves, by such readers as are not in too much haste, or busied and taken up with other concerns.

Narration and Discussion

Why does Plutarch think that Dionysius deliberately played a bit of a fool in Corinth?

If you have had a negative impression of Dionysius so far (as a tyrant king and an enemy of Timoleon), do these stories about him give you a different view? Was he someone you would like to have known? (Details about his rather strange upbringing and education are found in the *Life of Dion*.)

For older students: Plutarch says that some Corinthians saw in Dionysius's life "what great power, secret and divine causes have over men's weakness and frailty, and those things that daily passeth over our heads" (North's translation). Dryden translates that as "a proof of the strength and potency with which divine and unseen causes operate amidst the weakness of human visible things." Would Christians agree with this viewpoint?

Creative narration #1: Retell the first part of this lesson with the tabletop model.

Creative narration #2: The story of Dionysius in Corinth may inspire some dramatic interpretation, or perhaps a news interview.

Lesson Six

Introduction

The island fort had been taken by the Corinthians, but the rest of the city was dominated by Carthaginian troops, and food was getting low. However, Timoleon's "Fortune" seemed to be looking out for him.

Vocabulary

strange, wonderful: out of the normal course of things

set the Corinthians in such a jollity: pleased them so much

bestowed their leisure: spent their free time

resigned it up again: gave it back to them

diverting himself without any apprehension…: going among the people without any fear of harm

lofty precipice: high cliff or rock face

ten minas: a mina was an amount of money, equal to one-sixtieth of a **talent**; so ten minas would have been quite a large amount

good hap: good fortune

nicety: subtlety, stealth

subjugated: conquered

their victuals waxed scant: they were running out of food

straitly kept: tightly guarded

devised instruments and inventions: war machines

sally: a sudden charge out of a besieged place

dispersed abroad by tempest…: the ships guarding the fort had been driven out of formation by the wind and waves

Acradina: a residential section of Syracuse (see introductory notes)

precincts: boundaries

post: messenger

People

Mago, their admiral: a long-serving Carthaginian officer

On the Map

Thurians: those of the **Thurii** city/colony, on the Tarentine gulf

Brutians/Bruttians: modern-day Calabria

Catana: see introductory notes

Reading

Part One

But now if the tyrant Dionysius's wretched state seems **strange**, Timoleon's prosperity then was no less **wonderful**. For within fifty days after he had set foot in Sicily, he had the citadel of Syracuse in his possession, and sent Dionysius as an exile into Peloponnesus.

This did **set the Corinthians in such a jollity** that they sent him a supply of two thousand footmen and two hundred horsemen, which were appointed to land in Italy, in the country of the **Thurians**. And perceiving that they could not possibly go from thence into Sicily, because the Carthaginians kept the seas with a great navy of ships, and that thereby they were compelled to stay for a better opportunity: in the meantime, they **bestowed their leisure** in doing a notable good act. For the **Thurians**, going out to war against their **Bruttian** enemies, left their city in charge with these Corinthian strangers, who defended it as carefully as if it had been their own country, and [then] faithfully **resigned it up again**.

Part Two

Hicetas, all this while, did besiege the castle of Syracuse, preventing in every way possible that there should come no provisions by sea unto the Corinthians that kept within the castle. He had engaged also, and despatched towards Adranum, two unknown foreigners to assassinate Timoleon, who at no time kept any standing guard about his person, and was then altogether secure, **diverting himself without any apprehension among the citizens of the place**, it being a festival in honour of their gods. The two men that were sent, having casually heard that Timoleon was about to sacrifice, came directly into the temple with daggers under their cloaks, and pressing in among the crowd, by little and little got up close to the altar; but, as they were just looking for a sign from each other to begin the attempt, a third person struck one of them over the head with a sword, upon whose sudden fall neither he that gave the blow, nor the partisan of him that received it, kept their stations any longer; but the one, making way with his bloody sword, put no stop to his flight till he gained the top of a certain **lofty precipice**; while the other, laying hold of the altar, besought Timoleon to spare his life, and he would reveal to him the whole conspiracy. His pardon being granted, he confessed that both himself and his dead companion were both hired and sent to kill him.

While this discovery was made, he that killed the other conspirator had been fetched down from his sanctuary of the rock, loudly and often protesting, as he came along, that there was no injustice in the fact, as he had only taken righteous vengeance for his father's blood, whom this man had murdered before in the city of Leontini; the truth of which was attested by several there present, who could not choose but wonder too at the strange dexterity of Fortune's operations, the facility with which she makes one event the spring and motion to something wholly different, uniting every scattered accident and loose particular and remote action, and interweaving them together to serve her purpose; so that things that in themselves seem to have no connection or interdependence whatsoever, become in her hands, so to say, the end and the beginning of each other.

The Corinthians, examining this matter thoroughly, gave him that slew the soldier with his sword a crown of the value of **ten minas**, because that by means of his just anger, he had done good service to the god that had preserved Timoleon. And furthermore, this **good hap** did not only serve the present turn but was to good purpose ever after. For those that saw it were put in better hope, and they had thenceforth more care and regard unto Timoleon's person, because he was a holy man, one that loved the gods, and that was purposely sent to deliver Sicily from captivity.

Part Three

But Hicetas having missed his first purpose, and seeing numbers daily drawn to Timoleon's devotion: he was mad with himself, that having so great an army of the Carthaginians at hand at his commandment, he took but a few of them to serve his turn, as if he had been ashamed of his fact, and had used their friendship by stealth. Therefore, now laying aside his former **nicety**, he called in Mago, their admiral, with his whole navy, who presently set sail, and seized upon the port with a formidable fleet of at least a hundred and fifty vessels, landing there sixty thousand foot soldiers, which were all lodged within the city of Syracuse; so that, in all men's opinion, the time anciently talked of and long expected, wherein Sicily should be **subjugated** by barbarians, was now come to its fatal period. For in all their preceding wars and many desperate conflicts with Sicily, the Carthaginians had never been able, before this, to take Syracuse; whereas Hicetas now receiving them and putting them into their hands, you might see it become now, as it were, a camp of barbarians.

On the other side, the Corinthians that were within the castle found themselves in great distress, because **their victuals waxed scant**, and the haven was so **straitly kept**. Moreover, they were driven to be armed continually to defend the walls, which the enemies battered, and assaulted in sundry places, with all kinds of engines of battery, and sundry sorts of **devised instruments and inventions** to take cities: by reason whereof, they were compelled also to divide themselves into many companies. Timoleon made shift to relieve them in these [difficulties], sending corn from **Catana** by small fishing-boats and little skiffs, which commonly gained a passage through the Carthaginian galleys in times of storm, stealing up when the blockading ships were driven apart and dispersed by the stress of weather; which Mago and Hicetas observing, they agreed to fall upon Catana, from whence these supplies were brought in to the besieged; and taking with them the best soldiers of all their army, they departed from Syracuse, and sailed towards Catana.

Part Four

Now in the mean space, Neon the Corinthian, captain of those that kept the citadel, taking notice that the enemies who stayed there behind were very negligent and careless in keeping guard, made a sudden **sally** upon them as they lay scattered, and, killing some and putting others to flight, he took and possessed himself of that quarter which they called **Acradina**, and was thought to be the strongest and most impregnable part of Syracuse, a city made up and compacted, as it were, of several towns put together. Having thus stored himself with corn and money, he did not abandon the place, nor retire again into the castle, but fortifying the **precincts** of Acradina, and joining it by works to the citadel, he undertook the defense of both.

Now were Mago and Hicetas very near unto Catana, when a **post** overtook them, purposely sent from Syracuse unto them: who brought them news that the Acradina was taken. Whereat they both wondered, and returned back again with all speed possible (having failed of their purpose at Catana) to keep that which they had yet left in their hands.

Narration and Discussion

What were the results of Neon's observation about the castle guards?

Explain why people believed Timoleon must have had some kind of guardian angel (or "Fortune") looking after him. Do you agree with their thinking?

What person or group of people do you think showed the most courage or strength of character in this passage?

Creative narration #1: Use the model you made to retell the events of this lesson. (Things right now are a bit confused: Timoleon is in Adranum, but Hicetas is besieging the castle in Syracuse.)

Lesson Seven

Introduction

As the battle for Syracuse continued, the Corinthian backup troops found a way across to the island. A campaign to discourage the mercenaries working for the Carthaginians was also successful; but Hicetas was resolved to fight to the end, even if he had to do it alone.

Vocabulary

These successes, indeed, were such…: The success of the previous events could be credited to the skill and courage of those involved, with nothing supernatural about it.

Felicity: good luck and good fortune. According to Plutarch, the next event could only have occurred by intervention of the gods, or perhaps sheer luck (in contrast to **"These successes"**). (What is the difference between the deities **Fortuna** and **Felicitas**? **Fortuna** was thought to be unpredictable, as you can have good or bad fortune. But **Felicitas** was associated only with happiness or blessedness.)

tempestuous: stormy

policy: trick

trifling: playing around

barks: small boats

times of truce: times when there was no fighting

tarry: wait

Acradina, Epipolae: see introductory notes

People

Hanno: Hanno the Great of Carthage

Demaratus: a Corinthian military leader

On the Map

Messina: a city and its surrounding area on the Strait of Messina

Reading

Part One

These successes, indeed, were such as might leave Foresight and Courage a pretence still of disputing it with Fortune, which contributed most to the result. But the next following event can scarcely be ascribed to anything but pure **Felicity**.

The Corinthian soldiers who stayed at Thurii, partly for fear of the Carthaginian galleys which lay in wait for them under the command of **Hanno**, and partly because of **tempestuous** weather which had lasted for many days, and rendered the sea dangerous, took a resolution to march by land over the Bruttian territories, and what with persuasion and force together, made good their passage through those barbarians to the city of Rhegium, the sea being still rough and raging as before.

But Hanno, not expecting the Corinthians would venture out, and supposing it would be useless to wait there any longer, thought with himself that he had devised a marvellous fine **policy** to deceive the enemies. Thereupon he willed all his men to put garlands of flowers of triumph upon their heads, and therewithal also made them dress up, and adorned his galleys with bucklers, of both the Greek and Carthaginian make. So in this bravery he returned again, sailing towards Syracuse, and came in with force of rowers, rowing under the castle side of Syracuse, with great laughing, and clapping of hands: crying out aloud to them that were in the castle that he had overthrown their aid which came from Corinth as they thought to pass by the coast of Italy into Sicily; flattering themselves that this did much discourage those that were besieged.

While he was thus **trifling** and playing his tricks before Syracuse, the two thousand Corinthians, now come as far as Rhegium, observing the coast clear, and that the raging seas were by miracle (as it were) made of purpose calm for them: they took seas forthwith in such little **barks** and fishing boats as they found ready, in which they went into Sicily in such complete safety and in such an extraordinary calm, that they drew their horses by the reins, swimming along by them as the vessels went across. When they were all landed, Timoleon came to receive them, and by their means at once obtained possession of **Messina**, from whence he marched in good order to Syracuse, trusting more to his [recent] prosperous achievements than his present strength, as the whole army he had then with him did not exceed the number of four thousand.

Notwithstanding, Mago, hearing of his coming, quaked for fear, and doubted the more upon the following occasion. About Syracuse are certain marshes that receive great quantity of sweet fresh water, as well of fountains and springs, as also of little running brooks, lakes, and rivers, which run that way towards the sea: and, therefore, there are great store of eels in that place, and the fishing is great there at all times, but specially for such as delight to take eels. The mercenary soldiers that served on both sides were wont to follow the sport together at their vacant hours, and upon any cessation of arms; who being all Greeks, and having no cause of private enmity to each other, as they would venture bravely in fight, so in **times of truce** used to meet and converse amicably together.

And at this present time, while engaged about this common business of fishing, they fell into talk together; and some expressing their admiration of the neighbouring sea, and others telling how much they were taken with the convenience and commodiousness of the buildings and public works, one of the Corinthian party took occasion to demand of the others:

> "Is it possible that you that be Grecians born,
> and have so goodly a city [*meaning Syracuse*]
> of your own, and full of so many goodly
> commodities: that ye will give it up unto these
> barbarous people, the vile Carthaginians, and
> most cruel murderers of the world? Whereas
> you should rather wish that there were many
> Sicilies betwixt them and Greece. Have ye so
> little consideration or judgment to think that
> they have assembled an army out of all Africa,
> unto Hercules' Pillars, and to the sea Atlantic,
> to come hither to fight to stablish Hicetas'
> tyranny: who, if he had been a wise and skillful
> captain, would not have cast out his ancestors
> and founders to bring into his country the
> ancient enemies of the same: but might have
> received such honour and authority of the
> Corinthians and Timoleon, as he could
> reasonably have desired, and that with all their
> favour and good will?"

The Greeks that were in pay with Hicetas, noising these discourses about their camp, gave Mago some ground to suspect, as indeed he had long sought for a pretense to be gone, that there was treachery contrived against him; so that, although Hicetes entreated him to **tarry,** and made it appear how much stronger they were than the enemy, yet, conceiving they came far more short of Timoleon in respect of courage and fortune than they surpassed him in number, he presently went aboard and set sail for Africa, letting Sicily escape out of his hands with dishonour to himself, and for such uncertain causes, that no human reason could give an account of his departure.

Part Two

The next day after Mago was gone, Timoleon came up before the city in array for a battle. But when he and his company heard of this sudden flight, and saw the docks all empty, they then began to jest at Mago's cowardliness, and in mockery caused proclamation to be made through the city that a reward would be given to anyone who could bring them tidings whither the Carthaginian fleet had conveyed itself from them.

However, Hicetas resolving to fight it out alone, and not quitting his hold of the city, but sticking close to the quarters he was in possession of, places that were well fortified and not easy to be attacked, Timoleon divided his forces into three parts, and fell himself upon the side where the river Anapas ran, which was most strong and difficult of access; and he commanded those that were led by Isias, a Corinthian captain, to make their assault from the post of **Acradina**, while Dirachus and Demaretus, that brought him the last supply from Corinth, were, with a third division, to attempt the quarter called **Epipolae**. A considerable impression being made from every side at once, the soldiers of Hicetas were beaten off and put to flight; and this—that the city came to be taken by storm, and fall suddenly into their hands, upon the defeat and rout of the enemy—we must in all justice ascribe to the valour of the assailants and the wise conduct of their general. But where there was not one Corinthian slain, nor hurt in this assault: sure methinks herein, it was only the work and deed of Fortune, that did favour and protect Timoleon, to contend against his valiantness. To the end that those which should hereafter hear of his doings should have more occasion to wonder at his good hap, than to praise and commend his valiantness.

For the fame of this great exploit did in a few days not only run through all Italy, but also through all Greece. Insomuch as the Corinthians (who could scant believe their men were passed with safety into Sicily) understood withal that they were safely arrived there, and that they had gotten the victory of their enemies: so prosperous was their journey, and Fortune so speedily did favour his noble acts.

Narration and Discussion

How did Hanno's trick backfire on him?

Explain the speech of the Corinthian mercenary to those fighting on the Carthaginian side. What was its unexpected result?

For older students: It might be interesting (strictly for fun) to take on the role of Fortune and have her describe (a bit boastfully) the part she played in these events.

Creative narration #1: Use the model to show how Timoleon's forces finally took Syracuse.

Creative narration #2: Dramatize the "fishing for eels" scene.

Lesson Eight

Introduction

The Corinthians were now positioned to do whatever they wanted with Syracuse. They could install another tyrant king and control the region; but that was not their plan. With the support of the Corinthians, the Syracusans themselves began to rebuild their devastated city.

Vocabulary

> **the error of Dion:** Dion, who had seized the fortress to end the tyranny of Dionysius, and had then taken it for himself

> **mattock:** a tool like a pickaxe

> **suit:** request

hard by the walls: just outside the city walls

stout: strong

barren: empty, unused

in recompense: As reward or payment

repaired: went

a thousand talents: a talent was a weight of silver or gold. One talent was the equivalent (by one estimate) to what a skilled worker might earn in nine years.

defray the common charges: cover the expenses

statues or images: public statues

establishment of the commonweal: setting up the new government

Reading

Part One

Timoleon, having now the castle of Syracuse in his hands, did not follow **the error of Dion.** For he spared not the castle for the beauty and stately building thereof, but, avoiding the suspicion that caused Dion first to be accused, and lastly to be slain: he caused it to be proclaimed by trumpet, that any Syracusan whatsoever should come with pickaxes and **mattocks,** to help to dig down and overthrow the fort of the tyrants. When they all came up with one accord, looking upon that order and that day as the surest foundation of their liberty, they not only pulled down the castle, but overturned the palaces and monuments adjoining, and whatever else might preserve any memory of former tyrants. And having cleared the place in few days, and made all plain, Timoleon, at the **suit** of the citizens, made council-halls and places of justice to be built there: and did by this means establish a free state and popular government, and did suppress all tyrannical power.

However, he saw he had won a city that had no inhabitants, which wars before had consumed, and fear of tyranny had emptied, so as grass grew so high and rank in the great marketplace of Syracuse, as they grazed their horses there, and the horsekeepers lay down by them on the grass as they fed; and that all the cities, a few excepted, were full of red deer and wild boars, so that men given to delight in hunting, having leisure, might find game many times within the suburbs and town ditches, **hard by the walls**; and that such as dwelt in castles and strongholds in the country, would not leave them to come and dwell in cities, by reason they were all grown so **stout** and did so hate and detest assemblies of council, orations, and order of government, where so many tyrants had reigned.

Timoleon, therefore, with the Syracusans that remained, considering this vast desolation, and how little hope there was to have it otherwise supplied, thought good to write to the Corinthians, to send people out of Greece to inhabit the city of Syracuse again. For otherwise the country would grow **barren** and unprofitable, if the ground were not plowed. And besides this, they expected to be involved in a greater war from Africa, having news brought them that Mago had killed himself, and that the Carthaginians, out of rage for his ill-conduct in the late expedition, had caused his body to be nailed upon a cross; and that they were raising a mighty force, with design to make their descent upon Sicily the next summer.

Part Two

These letters of Timoleon being brought unto Corinth, and the ambassadors of Syracuse being arrived with them also, who besought the people to take care and protection over their poor city, and that they would once again be founders of the same: the Corinthians did not greedily desire to be lords of so goodly and great a city, but first proclaimed by the trumpet in all the assemblies, solemn feasts, and common plays of Greece, that the Corinthians having destroyed the tyranny that was in the city of Syracuse, and driven out the tyrants, did call the Syracusans that were fugitives out of their country home again, and all other Sicilians that liked to come and dwell there, to enjoy all freedom and liberty, with promise to make just and equal division of the lands among them, the one to have as much as the other.

Moreover, they sent out posts and messengers into Asia, and into all the lands where they understood the banished Syracusans remained: to persuade and entreat them to come to Corinth, promising that the

Corinthians would give them ships, captains, and means to conduct them safely unto Syracuse, at their own proper costs and charges. **In recompense** whereof, the city of Corinth received every man's most noble praise and blessing, as well for delivering Sicily in that sort from the bondage of tyrants: as also for keeping it out of the hands of the barbarous people, and restored the natural Syracusans and Sicilians to their home and country again.

Nevertheless, such Sicilians as **repaired** to Corinth upon this proclamation (themselves being but a small number to inhabit the country) besought the Corinthians to join to them some other inhabitants as well of Corinth itself, as out of the rest of Greece: the which was performed. For they gathered together about ten thousand persons, whom they shipped and sent to Syracuse; where there were already a great number of others come unto Timoleon, as well out of Sicily itself, as out of all Italy besides: so that (as Athanis reports) their entire body amounted now to sixty thousand men.

Amongst them he divided the whole country, and sold them houses of the city, unto the value of **a thousand talents**. And because he would leave the old Syracusans able to recover their own, and to make the poor people by this means to have money in common, to **defray the common charges** of the city, as also their expenses in time of wars: the **statues or images** were sold, and the people by most voices did condemn them [the statues]. For they were solemnly indicted, accused, and arraigned, as if they had been men alive to be condemned. And it is reported that the Syracusans did reserve the statue of Gelon, an ancient tyrant of their city, honouring his memory, because of a great victory he had won of the Carthaginians, near the city of Himera; but they condemned all the rest to be taken away out of every corner of the city, and to be sold.

Part Three

Thus began the city of Syracuse to replenish again, and by little and little to recover itself, many people coming from all parts to dwell there. Thereupon Timoleon thought to set all the other cities at liberty also, and utterly to root out all the tyrants of Sicily: and to obtain his purpose, he went to make wars with them at their own doors. The first he went against was Hicetes, whom he compelled to forsake the league of the Carthaginians, and to promise also that he would raze all the fortresses he kept, and to live like a private man within the city of the Leontines *[omission for length]*. When he had brought this to pass, he returned forthwith to Syracuse about the **establishment of the commonweal**, assisting Cephalus and Dionysius, two notable men sent from Corinth to reform the laws, and to help them to stablish the goodliest ordinances for their commonweal.

Narration and Discussion

Show how Timoleon demonstrated wisdom in his dealings with the Syracusans. How did the people of Corinth help?

How did the Syracusans raise money to restore their city?

For further thought: Why didn't the Syracusans who "dwelt in castles and strongholds in the country" want to return? How might Timoleon have related to this feeling?

Creative narration #1: Use the model to illustrate the destruction of the castle, and the arrival of new inhabitants in Syracuse. In preparation for the next lesson, you may want to mark the city of Lilybaeum, on the western coast of Sicily.

Creative narration #2: Write the thoughts of a Syracusan witnessing the sale of his favourite statue.

Creative narration #3: Interview one of the new arrivals (or have him/her write a letter home).

Lesson Nine

Introduction

Timoleon banished some of the former tyrants to Corinth, and he confined Hicetas to Leontini, with the condition that he stay out of military involvement. Hicetas and his allies were still determined to rule

Sicily, however, and even more so when they heard that the Corinthians had moved into Carthaginian territory.

Vocabulary

promontory: a point of land jutting out into the water

by piecemeal and in parts: bit by bit

their country: their territory

rash: foolishly bold

if they fell upon it: if they were killed

he had that proof of them: they showed their true natures before he had to depend on them in battle

sepulchers of the dead: tombs

talons: claws

formidable: large, powerful

throng for passage: push to get through

ford: cross

in the flank: on each side

vanguard: those at the front

People

Hasdrubal and **Hamilcar:** Carthaginian generals

Demaratus: see **Lesson Seven**

Historic Occasions

340-339 B.C.: Hicetas persuaded Carthage to send troops to Lilybaeum

339 B.C.: Battle of the Crimissus

On the Map

Lilybaeum: a Phoenician city on the western coast of Sicily; the site of
present-day Marsala. The Phoenician name, translated as
"Lilybaeum" in Latin, meant "Town that Looks on Libya."

Crimissus: possibly the Freddo, a river in northwestern Sicily

Reading

Part One

And now in the meantime, because the soldiers had a mind to get
something of their enemies, and to avoid idleness, he sent them out
abroad to a country subject to the Carthaginians, under the charge of
Dinachus and Demaretus: where they made many little towns rebel
against the barbarous people, and did not only live in abundance of
wealth, but they gathered money together also to maintain the wars.

Meantime, the Carthaginians landed at the **promontory** of
Lilybaeum, bringing with them an army of seventy thousand men on
board two hundred galleys, besides a thousand other vessels laden with
engines of battery, chariots, corn, and other military stores, as if they
did not intend to manage the war **by piecemeal and in parts** as
heretofore, but to drive the Greeks altogether and at once out of all
Sicily. For indeed it was an able army to overcome all the Sicilians, if
they had been whole of themselves, and not divided.

Now they being advertised that the Sicilians had invaded **their
country**, they went towards them in great fury, led by **Hasdrubal** and
Hamilcar, generals of the army. This news was straight brought to
Syracuse, and the inhabitants were so stricken with fear of the report
of their army: that although there were a marvellous great number of
them within the city, scant three thousand of them had the hearts to
arm themselves, and to go to the field with Timoleon. The foreigners,
serving for pay, were not above four thousand in all, and about a
thousand of these grew faint-hearted by the way, and forsook
Timoleon in his march towards the enemy. They said that Timoleon
was out of his wits and more **rash** than his years required, to undertake,
with five thousand footmen and a thousand horse, to go against

seventy thousand men: and besides, to carry that small force he had to defend himself withal, eight great days' journey from Syracuse. So, that if it chanced they were compelled to flee, they would have no retreat, nor any burial **if they fell upon it**. Nevertheless, Timoleon was glad **he had that proof of them** before he came to battle. Moreover, having encouraged those that remained with him, he made them march with speed towards the river **Crimissus**, where he understood he should meet with the Carthaginians.

As he was marching up an ascent, from the top of which they expected to have a view of the army and of the strength of the enemy, there met him by chance a train of mules loaded with parsley; which his soldiers conceived to be an ominous occurrence or ill-boding token, because this is the herb with which we not unfrequently adorn the **sepulchers of the dead**; and there is a proverb derived from the custom, used of one who is dangerously sick, that "he has need of nothing but parsley."

But Timoleon to draw them from this foolish superstition and ease their minds, stayed the army. And when he had used certain persuasions unto them, according to the time, his leisure, and the occasion: he told them that the garland of itself came to offer them victory beforehand. "For," said he, "the Corinthians do crown them that win the Isthmian games (which are celebrated in their country) with garlands of parsley." And at that time also even in the solemn Isthmian games, they used the garland of parsley for reward and token of victory; and at this present it is also used in the games of Nemea [omission].

Part Two

Now when Timoleon had thus encouraged his men, as you have heard before, he took of this parsley, and made himself a garland, and put it on his head. When they saw that, the captains and all the soldiers also took of the same and made themselves the like. The soothsayers then, observing also two eagles on the wing towards them, one of which bore a snake struck through with her **talons**, and the other, as she flew, uttered a loud cry indicating boldness and assurance, at once showed them to the soldiers, who did then all together with one voice call upon the gods for help.

Timoleon

It was now about the beginning of the summer (and towards the end of the month called Thargelion, not far from the solstice), when there rose a great mist out of the river that covered all the fields over, so as they could not see the enemies' camp, but only heard a marvellous confused noise of men's voices, as if it had come from a great army; and, rising up to the top of the hill, they laid their targets down on the ground to take a little breath. The sun having drawn and sucked up all the moist vapours of the mist unto the top of the hills, the air began to be so thick that the tops of the mountains were all covered over with clouds; and, contrarily, the valley underneath was all clear and fair, that they might easily see the River Crimissus, and the enemies also, passing over it, first with their **formidable** four-horse chariots of war, and then ten thousand footmen bearing white shields, whom they guessed to be all Carthaginians, from the splendour of their arms, and the slowness and order of their march.

And when now the troops of various other nations, flowing in behind them, began to **throng for passage** in a tumultuous and unruly manner, Timoleon, perceiving that the river gave them opportunity to single off whatever number of their enemies they had a mind to engage at once, and bidding his soldiers observe how their forces were divided into two separate bodies by the intervention of the stream, some being already over, and others still to **ford** it, gave Demaretus command to fall in upon the Carthaginians with his horse, and disturb their ranks before they should be drawn up into form of battle; and coming down into the plain himself, forming his right and left wing of other Sicilians, intermingling only a few strangers in each, he placed the native of Syracuse in the middle, with the stoutest mercenaries he had about his own person; and waiting a little to observe the actions of his horse, when he saw they were not only hindered from grappling with the Carthaginians by the armed chariots that ran to and fro before the army, but forced continually to wheel about to escape having their ranks broken, and so to repeat their charges anew. Wherefore Timoleon taking his target on his arm, cried out aloud to his footmen, to follow him courageously, and to fear nothing. Those that heard his voice, thought it more than the voice of a man, whether the fury of his desire to fight did so strain it beyond ordinary course, or that some god (as many thought it then) did stretch his voice to cry out so loud and sensibly.

When his soldiers quickly gave an echo to it, and besought him to lead them on without any further delay, he made a sign to the horse, that they should draw off from the front where the chariots were, and pass sidewards to attack their enemies **in the flank**; then, making his **vanguard** firm by joining man to man and target to target, he caused the trumpet to sound, and so bore in upon the Carthaginians.

Narration and Discussion

Discuss the story of the load of parsley. How did Timoleon use it to turn his men from fear to courage?

Explain the strategy that Timoleon planned to use against the Carthaginians. How did he show skill in leadership, especially in dealing with the problem of the chariots?

Creative narration #1: You may choose to use the tabletop map or model, although this story takes place in a new location and may require some extra setup.

Creative narration #2: Dramatize the story of a) Timoleon and the parsley, or b) the battle so far at the Crimissus.

Lesson Ten

Introduction

This lesson continues the story of the Battle of the Crimissus, and its aftermath.

Vocabulary

onset: attack

without cessation: without stopping

stood the Grecians to great purpose: helped them a great deal

without any certain channel: without any proper outlet

spoils: loot, treasure, plunder; especially from a defeated enemy.

stood not trifling: did not bother

commended: praised, applauded

basely: dishonourably, shamefully

made a league: made an alliance, joined forces

to hazard all: to risk everything

sacrilege: an unholy act

People

Gisgo: the son of Hanno the Great

Reading

Part One

The Carthaginians, for their part, stoutly received and sustained Timoleon's first **onset**; and having their bodies armed with breast-plates of iron, and helmets of brass on their heads, besides great bucklers to cover and secure them, they could easily repel the charge of the Greek spears.

But when they came to handle their swords, where agility was more requisite than force, a fearful tempest of thunder, and flashing lightning withal, came from the mountains. After that came dark thick clouds also (gathered together from the top of the hills); and then fell upon the valley where the battle was fought a marvellous extreme shower of rain, fierce violent winds, and hail withal. All this tempest was upon the Grecians' backs, but discharged itself in the very faces of the barbarians, the rain beating on them, and the lightning dazzling them **without cessation**; annoyances that in many ways distressed at any rate the inexperienced, who had not been used to such hardships; and, in particular, the claps of thunder, and the noise of the rain and hail beating on their arms, kept them from hearing the commands of their officers.

Moreover, the mud did as much annoy the Carthaginians, because they were not nimble in their armour, but heavily armed as we have told you; and besides that, also, when the plates of their coats were thoroughly wet with water, they did load and hinder them so much the more that they could not fight with any ease. This **stood the Grecians to great purpose**, to throw them down the easier. Thus, when they were tumbling in the mud with their heavy armour, up they could rise no more.

Furthermore, the River Crimissus being risen high through the great rage of waters, and also for the multitude of people that passed over it, it did overflow the valley all about: which being full of ditches, many caves, and hollow places, it was straight all drowned over, and filled with many running streams, that ran overthwart the field, **without any certain channel**. The Carthaginians being compassed all about with these waters, they could hardly find their way out of it.

So as in the end, they being overcome with the storm that still did beat upon them, and the Grecians having slain many of their men at the first onset, to the number of four hundred of their choicest men, who made the first front of their battle: all the rest of their army turned their backs immediately, and fled for life.

Great numbers were overtaken in the plain, and put to the sword there; and many of them, as they were making their way back through the river, falling foul upon others that were yet coming over, were borne away and overwhelmed by the waters; but the major part, attempting to get up the hill so as to make their escape, were intercepted and destroyed by the light-armed troops. It is said that, of ten thousand who lay dead after the fight, three thousand, at least, were Carthaginian citizens; a heavy loss and great grief to their countrymen; those that fell being men inferior to none among them as to birth, wealth, or reputation. Nor do their records mention that so many native Carthaginians were cut off before in any one battle *[omission]*.

The Greeks easily discovered of what condition and account the slain were by the richness of their **spoils**. For they that spoiled them **stood not trifling** about getting of copper and iron together, because they found gold and silver enough. Passing over the river they became masters of their camp and carriages. As for captives, a great many of them were stolen away and sold privately by the soldiers; but about five thousand were brought in and delivered up for the benefit of the public; two hundred of their chariots of war were also taken.

The tent of Timoleon then presented a most glorious and magnificent appearance, being heaped up and hung round with every variety of spoils and military ornaments, among which were a thousand breastplates of rare workmanship and beauty, and bucklers to the number of ten thousand. The victors being but few to strip so many that were vanquished, and having such valuable spoils to occupy them, it was the third day after the fight before they could erect and finish the trophy of their conquest.

Then Timoleon sent unto Corinth, with the news of this overthrow, the fairest armours that were gotten in the spoil: because he would make his country and native city spoken of and **commended** through the world, above all the other cities of Greece. For that at Corinth only, their chief temples were set forth and adorned, not with spoils of the Grecians, nor offerings gotten by spilling the blood of their own nation and country (which to say truly, are unpleasant memories), but with the spoils taken from the barbarous people their enemies, with inscriptions witnessing the valiancy and justice of those also who by victory had obtained them. That is, to wit, that the Corinthians and their captain Timoleon (having delivered the Grecians dwelling in Sicily from the bondage of the Carthaginians) had given those offerings unto the gods, to give thanks for their victory.

Part Two

Having done this, Timoleon left his hired soldiers in the enemy's country to drive and carry away all they could throughout the subject-territory of Carthage, and so marched with the rest of his army to Syracuse, where he issued an edict for banishing the thousand mercenaries who had **basely** deserted him before the battle, and obliged them to quit the city before sunset. They, sailing into Italy, lost their lives there by the hands of the Bruttians, in spite of a public assurance of safety previously given them; thus receiving, from the divine power, a just reward of their own treachery.

Mamercus, however, the tyrant of Catana, and Hicetas, after all, either envying Timoleon the glory of his exploits, or fearing him as one that would keep no agreement or have any peace with tyrants, **made a league** with the Carthaginians, and pressed them much to send a new army and commander into Sicily, unless they would be content **to hazard all** and to be wholly ejected out of that island.

And in consequence of this, **Gisgo** was despatched with a navy of seventy sail. He took numerous Greek mercenaries also into pay, that being the first time they had ever been enlisted for the Carthaginian service; but then it seems the Carthaginians began to admire them, as men invincible, and the best soldiers of the world.

Part Three (optional)

Moreover, the inhabitants of the territory of Messina, having made a secret conspiracy amongst themselves, did slay four hundred men that Timoleon had sent unto them; and in the territories subject unto the Carthaginians, near unto a place they call Hierae, there was another ambush laid for Euthymus the Leucadian, so as himself and all his soldiers were cut in pieces. Howbeit the loss of them made Timoleon's doings accounted all the more remarkable, as these four hundred were the men that, with Philomelus of Phocis and Onomarchus, had forcibly broken into the temple of Apollo at Delphi, and were partakers with them in the **sacrilege**; so that being hated and shunned by all, as persons under a curse, they had been constrained to wander about in Peloponnesus; when, for want of others, Timoleon was glad to take them into service in his expedition for Sicily, where they were successful in whatever enterprise they attempted under his conduct.

But now, when all the important dangers were past, on his sending them out for the relief and defense of his party in several places, they perished and were destroyed at a distance from him, not all together, but in small parties; and the vengeance which was destined for them, so accommodating itself to the good fortune which guarded Timoleon as not to allow any harm or prejudice for good men to arise from the punishment of the wicked. The benevolence and kindness which the gods had for Timoleon was thus as distinctly recognized in his disasters as in his successes.

[omission for length]

Narration and Discussion

How did bad weather help Timoleon's soldiers win the battle?

For older students: Why did Timoleon seem to feel the killing of four hundred soldiers in Messina was no great loss? Do you agree?

For older students and further thought: The pieces of Carthaginian armour that the Corinthians sent back to Greece were given "inscriptions witnessing the valiancy and justice of those also, who by victory had obtained them." Dryden translates this "the noblest titles inscribed upon them, titles telling of the justice as well as fortitude of the conquerors." What do you think Plutarch means by "justice?"

Creative narration #1: Use the tabletop model to tell about the battle.

Creative narration #2: Imagine a conversation between a Carthaginian army recruiter and some out-of-work Greek soldiers. How might he encourage them to join his side?

Lesson Eleven

Introduction

Although a few diehard tyrants (Hicetas and Mamercus) continued to struggle against Timoleon, it was obvious—even to them—that they had lost their support.

Vocabulary

havoc: destruction, damage

contention and dispute: quarrel, argument

onset: attack

pretenders: competitors

zealous: passionate, energetic

device: involvement; literally, his personal stamp

impute: credit

broils and tumults: conflicts

Historic Occasions

338 B.C.: Carthaginians agreed to peace terms

On the Map

Calauria [Kalaureia]: this appears not to be the island by that name near mainland Greece, but a city or town of Sicily.

Damyrias: also spelled Damurias; a river of Sicily

Agrigentum and **Gela:** cities on the southern coast of Sicily

Ceos [Kea]: an island in the Aegean Sea

Reading

Part One

After this, while Timoleon marched to **Calauria**, Hicetas made an inroad into the borders of Syracuse, where he carried away a marvellous great spoil. And having done much mischief and **havoc**, he returned back again, and came by Calauria to spite Timoleon, knowing well enough he had at that time but few men about him. Timoleon suffered him to pass by, but followed him afterwards with his horsemen and lightest armed footmen. Hicetas, understanding that, passed over the river called **Damyrias**, and so stayed on the other side as though he would fight, trusting to the swift running of the river and the height and steepness of the bank on each side, giving advantage enough to make him confident.

A strange **contention and dispute**, meantime, among the officers of Timoleon a little delayed the battle; none of them was willing to let another pass over before him to engage the enemy; each man claiming it as a right to venture first and begin the **onset**; so that their fording was likely to be tumultuous and without order, a mere general struggle which should be the foremost.

Timoleon, therefore, desiring to decide the quarrel by lot, took a ring from each of the **pretenders**, which he cast into his own cloak, and, after he had shaken all together, the first he drew out had, by good fortune, the figure of a trophy engraved as a seal upon it; at the sight of which the young captains all shouted for joy, and, without waiting any longer to see how chance would determine it for the rest, took every man his way through the river with all the speed they could make, and fell to blows with the enemies, who were not able to bear up against the violence of their attack, but fled in haste and left their weapons behind them all alike, and a thousand dead upon the place.

And within a few days after, Timoleon, leading his army to the city of the Leontines, took Hicetas alive there, with his son Eupolemus, and Euthymus, the general of his horsemen; who were delivered into his hands by Hicetas' own soldiers. Hicetas and his son were then executed as tyrants and traitors; and Euthymus, though a brave man, and one of singular courage, could obtain no mercy, because he was charged with certain injurious words he spoke against the Corinthians.

[Omission: the murder by the Syracusans of the wives and daughters of Hicetas, in revenge for a similar act against Dion. Mamercus (the tyrant of Catana) continued to conspire against Timoleon but was eventually caught and executed.]

Part Two

Thus did Timoleon cut the nerves of tyranny and put a period to the wars; and, whereas, at his first entering into Sicily, the island was as it were become wild again, and was hateful to the very natives on account of the evils and miseries they suffered there, he so civilized and restored it, and rendered it so desirable to all men, that even strangers now came by sea to inhabit those towns and places which their own citizens had formerly forsaken and left desolate. **Agrigentum** and **Gela**, two great cities that had been ruined and laid waste by the Carthaginians after the Attic war, were then peopled again, the one by Megellus and Pheristus from Elea, the other by Gorgus from the island of **Ceos**, partly with new settlers, partly with the old inhabitants whom they collected again from various parts; to all of whom Timoleon not only afforded a secure and peaceful abode after so obstinate a war, but was further so **zealous** in assisting and providing for them that he was honoured among them as their father and founder. And this his good love and favour was common also to all other people of Sicily whatsoever.

So that in all Sicily there was no truce taken in wars, nor laws established, nor lands divided, nor institution of any policy or government thought good or available, if Timoleon's **device** had not been in it, as chief director of such matters: which gave him a singular grace to be acceptable to the gods, and generally to be beloved of all men.

[short omission]

Part Three

For as the poetry of Antimachus, and painting of Dionysius, the artists of Colophon, though full of force and vigour, yet appeared to be strained and elaborate in comparison with the pictures of Nicomachus and the verses of Homer, which, besides, their general strength and beauty, have the peculiar charm of seeming to have been executed with perfect ease and readiness; even so in like manner, whosoever will compare the painful bloody wars and battles of Epaminondas and Agesilaus with the wars of Timoleon, in the which, besides equity and justice, there is also great ease and quietness: he shall find, weighing things indifferently, that they have not been Fortune's doings simply, but that they came of a most noble and "fortunate" courage. Yet Timoleon himself doth wisely **impute** it unto his good hap and favourable fortune (or the favour of Fortune). For in letters he wrote unto his familiar friends at Corinth, and in some other orations he made to the people of Syracuse: he [said] many times that he thanked the almighty gods, that it had pleased them to save and deliver Sicily from bondage by his means and service, and to give him the honour and dignity of the name.

And having built a temple in his house, he did dedicate it unto Fortune, and, furthermore, did consecrate his whole house unto her.

For he dwelt in a house which the Syracusans had selected for him, as a special reward and monument of his brave exploits, granting him together with it the most agreeable and beautiful piece of land in the whole country, where he kept his residence for the most part, and enjoyed a private life with his wife and children, who came to him from Corinth. For he returned thither no more, unwilling to be concerned in the **broils and tumults** of Greece, or to expose himself to public envy (the fatal mischief which great commanders continually run into, from the insatiable appetite for honours and authority); but wisely chose to spend the remainder of his days in Sicily, and there partake of the blessings he himself had procured, the greatest of which was to behold so many cities flourish, and so many thousands of people live happy through his means.

Narration and Discussion

Describe the events at the Damyrias River. How might it have ended badly? How did Timoleon handle the situation?

Why did Timoleon choose to stay in Sicily?

For older students: Why did Timoleon give so much credit to Fortune and the gods for his success? (Compare with Isaiah 45:1 and Acts 17:23.)

For further thought: In his comparison of Timoleon with Aemilius Paulus, Plutarch says "I would not intend any reflection on Timoleon for accepting of a house and handsome estate in the country…there is no dishonour in accepting; but yet there is greater glory in a refusal, and the supremest virtue is shown in not wanting what it might fairly take." Do you agree that it might have been more honourable to refuse the reward?

Creative narration #1: The dispute by the river Damyrias might lend itself to dramatic recreation.

Creative narration #2: Update the tabletop model to show how things stood after the wars; or, make a before-and-after drawing of

Sicily (from a "hateful" place to one which was being repopulated); or, do a news interview discussing how things have changed.

Lesson Twelve

Introduction:

Timoleon had to face a few harsh critics, but he handled them (as usual) with strength and grace. Plutarch ends the story with a description of Timoleon's final days in Syracuse.

Vocabulary

sureties: pledges, usually made with money

indictment: a formal charge

incensed: angry

rhetoricians: speechmakers

peradventure: perhaps

litter: a bed or seat that could be carried

propound the matter doubtful: explain the difficulty

colonnade: a series of columns, usually supporting a roof

People

Simonides: Simonides of Ceos, a Greek lyric poet

Laphystius, Demaenetus: enemies of Timoleon

Historic Occasions

337 B.C.: the death of Timoleon

336 B.C.: Alexander the Great became king of Macedon (for reference only)

Reading

Part One

As, however, not only, as **Simonides** says, "on every lark must grow a crest," but also in every democracy there must spring up a false accuser, so was it at Syracuse: two of their popular spokesmen, Laphystius and Demaenetus by name, fell to slander Timoleon. The former of whom requiring him to put in **sureties** that he would answer to an **indictment** that would be brought against him, Timoleon would not suffer the citizens, who were **incensed** at this demand, to oppose it or hinder the proceeding, since he of his own accord had been, he said, at all that trouble, and run so many dangerous risks for this very end and purpose, that everyone who wished to try matters by law should freely have recourse to it.

And when Demaenetus, in a full audience of the people, laid several things to his charge which had been done while he was general, he made no other reply to him, but only said he was much indebted to the gods for granting the request he had so often made them, namely, that he might live to see the Syracusans enjoy that liberty of speech which they now seemed to be masters of.

Now Timoleon, in all men's opinion, had done the noblest acts that ever a Grecian captain did in his time, and had above deserved the fame and glory of all the noble exploits which the **rhetoricians** with all their eloquent orations persuaded the Grecians unto, in the open assemblies, and common feasts and plays of Greece, out of the which Fortune delivered him safe and sound before the trouble of the civil wars that followed soon after; and moreover he made a great proof of his valiancy and knowledge in wars, against the barbarous people and tyrants, and had [shown] himself also a just and merciful man unto all his friends, and generally to all the Grecians.

And furthermore, seeing he won the most part of all his victories and triumphs without the shedding of any one tear of his men, or that any of them mourned by his means; and that he also rid all Sicily of all the miseries and calamities reigning at that time, in less than eight years' space: he being now grown old, his sight first beginning a little to fail him, shortly after he lost it altogether. Not that he had done anything himself which might occasion this, or was he deprived of his sight by any outrage of Fortune; it seems rather to have been some inbred and hereditary weakness that was founded in natural causes, which by length of time came to discover itself. For it is said, that several of his kindred and family were subject to the like gradual decay, and lost all use of their eyes, as he did, in their declining years.

[short omission]

Now, that he patiently took this misfortune to be blind altogether, **peradventure** men may somewhat marvel at it: but this much more is to be wondered at, that the Syracusans after he was blind, did so much honour him, and acknowledge the good he had done them, that they went themselves to visit him oft, and brought strangers (that were travelers) to his house in the city, and also in the country, to make them see their benefactor, rejoicing and thinking themselves happy that he had chosen to end his life with them, and that for this cause he had despised the glorious return that was prepared for him in Greece, for the great and happy victories he had won in Sicily. But amongst many other things the Syracusans did, and ordained to honour him with, this of all other methinketh was the chiefest: that they made a perpetual law [that] so oft as they should have wars against foreign people, and not against their own countrymen, that they should ever choose a Corinthian for their general.

It was a goodly thing also to see how they did honour him in the assemblies of their council. For if any trifling matter fell in question among them, they dispatched it of themselves: but if it were a thing that required great counsel and advice, they caused Timoleon to be sent for. So he was brought through the marketplace in his **litter**, into the theatre, where all the assembly of the people was, and carried in even so in his litter as he sat: and then the people did all salute him with one voice, and he them in like case. And after he had paused a while to hear the praises and blessings the whole assembly gave him, they did **propound the matter doubtful** to him, and he delivered his opinion upon the same: which being passed by the voices of the people, his servants carried him back again in his litter through the theatre, and the citizens did wait on him a little way with cries of joy, and clapping of hands, and that done, they did [return] to dispatch common causes by themselves, as they did before.

Part Two

So, his old age being thus entertained with such honour, and with the love and good will of every man, as of a common father to them all: in the end a sickness took him by the back, whereof he died.

The Syracusans had a certain time appointed them to prepare for his funeral, and their neighbours also thereabouts to come unto it. By reason whereof his funeral was so much more honourably performed in all things, and specially for that the people appointed the noblest young gentlemen of the city to carry his coffin upon their shoulders, richly furnished and set forth, whereon his body lay; and so did convey him through the place where the palace and castle of Dionysius stood before they were demolished by Timoleon.

There attended on the solemnity several thousands of men and women, all crowned with flowers, and arrayed in fresh and clean attire, which made it look like the procession of a public festival; and all their words were praisings and blessings of the dead, with tears running down their cheeks, which was a good testimony they did not this as men that were glad to be discharged of the honour they did him, neither for that it was so ordained: but for the just sorrow and grief they took for his death, and for very hearty good love they did bear him.

And lastly, the coffin being put upon the stack of wood where it should be burnt, one of the heralds that had the loudest voice proclaimed the decree that was ordained by the people, the effect whereof was this:

"The people of Syracuse hath ordained that this present body of Timoleon the Corinthian, the Son of Timodemus, should be buried at the charges of the commonweal, unto the sum of two hundred minas; and hath honoured his memory with plays and games of music, with running of horses, and with other exercises of the body, which shall be celebrated yearly on the day of his death for evermore; and this, because he did drive the tyrants out of Sicily, for that he overcame the barbarous people, and because he replenished many great cities with inhabitants again, which the wars had left desolate and unhabited; and lastly, for that he had restored the Sicilians again to their liberty, and allowed them to live after their own laws."

Besides this, they made a tomb for him in the marketplace, which they afterwards built round with **colonnades**, and attached to it places of exercise for the young men; and they gave it the name of the Timoleonteum. And keeping to that form and order of civil policy and observing those laws and constitutions which he left them, they lived themselves a long time in great prosperity.

Narration and Discussion

Why did Timoleon say he was glad to hear criticism of his military actions?

In what ways did the Syracusans show their admiration for Timoleon?

For older students: As a citizen, what does it mean to "frankly use the liberty of [your country's] laws?"

Creative narration: As a reporter, interview people in the crowd at Timoleon's funeral; or write about it for the "Sicily Times."

Examination Questions

Younger Students:

1. Why did Timoleon first save his brother's life and then consent to his death? Tell the whole story.

2. Give a short account of Timoleon's expedition against the Carthaginians.

Older Students:

1. Describe the conquest of Syracuse. How did Timoleon treat the city?

Bibliography

Plutarch's Lives of the Noble Greeks and Romans. Englished by Sir Thomas North. With an introduction by George Wyndham. Second Volume. London: Dent, 1894. (Timoleon)

Plutarch's Lives of the Noble Greeks and Romans. Englished by Sir Thomas North. With an introduction by George Wyndham. Fourth Volume. London: Dent, 1894. (Alexander)

Plutarch's Lives: The Dryden Plutarch. Revised by Arthur Hugh Clough. Volume 2. London: J.M. Dent, 1910. (Timoleon)

Plutarch's Lives: The Dryden Plutarch. Revised by Arthur Hugh Clough. Volume 4. Philadelphia: John D. Morris, 1860. (Alexander)

A helpful book of maps:

Hyslop, Stephen G., and Patricia Daniels. 2011. *Great empires: an illustrated atlas.* Washington, D.C.: National Geographic.
.

Made in the USA
Middletown, DE
15 October 2023

40810244R00106